Mother Shadow

Cynthia Banham

Cynthia Banham PhD is a full-time writer and part-time habitat gardener.

Previously, she worked as a lawyer, journalist and academic. She spent two decades in Canberra, initially working in the Federal Parliamentary Press Gallery and later completing a PhD on human rights law and politics at the Australian National University.

Since returning to Sydney, she has become immersed in restoring her manicured, suburban garden into a wilder place of refuge for frogs, lizards, insects, and small birds.

Cynthia Banham

Mother Shadow

A Meditation on Maternal Inheritance

First published in Australia in 2026
by Upswell Publishing
Perth, Western Australia
upswellpublishing.com

Upswell operates in the city of Perth, on ancient country of the Whadjuk people of the Noongar nation who remain the spiritual and cultural custodians of this beautiful land. We acknowledge their continuing connection to country and express gratitude to elders past and present for their strength and creativity...Always was, always will be, Aboriginal land.

ISBN: 978-1-7642397-1-4

A catalogue record for this book is available from the National Library of Australia

Cover design by Chil3, Fremantle
Typeset in Foundry Origin by Lasertype
Printed by McPherson's Printing Group

Upswell Publishing is assisted by the State of Western Australia through its funding program for arts and culture.

For L

Contents

1
Judgement

My mother always told me her Nonna Lina was an orphan. This was where our maternal line began, with a parentless girl from Bologna whose first name, Natalina, meant 'Christmas'.

I had assumed, since my mother knew nothing more of her grandmother's origins, that the girl's parents must have died before she had the chance to know them. Perhaps they both perished in an accident, though what kind – this was 1898 and they were poor – I never pondered. Nothing more was knowable, I reasoned; the dead parents were lost to the murk of time. I never imagined there had been a mother, still living, unknown to Natalina. A father too.

Then I found my great-grandmother's birth record. The year was 2017. The document was among a pile of family papers belonging to Natalina's last surviving daughter. Nobody else in the family wanted them and, since I have an interest in this sort of thing, I saved them from the rubbish heap.

The birth record was yellowed, two pages long, and the bottom right-hand corner was missing. At first, I was tickled to read her birthdate: 23 December, the day before Christmas Eve. It explained her pretty name. The record also informed me where she was born: in a house on a street named for the abbot, Via Abate, in a town I had never heard of called San Giovanni in Persiceto, somewhere in the fecund plains outside Bologna.

I read down to the end of the first page until one of the last lines pulled me up. Those jarring words: *che non consente di essere nominata*, 'who does not consent to be named'. They were her mother's words, and I hadn't been expecting them. Natalina, this told me, was not an orphan at all. Her mother had not died in childbirth or shortly after. Instead, she had not recognised her daughter as her own. For reasons I could not have explained at the time, this circumstance struck me as far more tragic than had both of Natalina's parents been killed in an industrial accident or a natural disaster.

Another word, over the page, informed me why her mother had not wanted to be named on the birth certificate: *brefotrofio*. I had to look it up. An Italian Wikipedia search enlightened: an institution, distinguished from an orphanage, 'that takes in and raises illegitimate, abandoned and unrecognised infants at birth or in danger of abandonment' (my translation). In short, a *brefotrofio* is a foundling home. The provincial official who recorded Natalina's birth ordered the baby be dispatched to the foundling home in Bologna and charged the midwife who oversaw her birth, Rosa Rizzi, with the task.

It made sense now. The mother was unmarried. Her daughter was illegitimate. She had abandoned her.

My impulse, when I understood the significance of those words, 'who does not consent to be named', was to assume some degree of maternal indifference, that the mother had cast off her daughter because she did not want her. Natalina, the unwanted Christmas gift. By withholding her name from her daughter's official papers, the woman consigned her to a life as a 'child of nobody'.

I experienced a kind of wild indignation on behalf of my great-grandmother. The missing corner of the birth document took on a new significance. Someone had clearly torn it off. Reading her birth record for the first time as an adult – Natalina needed it to marry my great-grandfather in 1923 – she would have seen in stark black and white her mother's renunciation of her. I imagined that she must have ripped the thick paper in a rage of angry tears, reducing the small triangular segment to a pile of tiny pieces.

I later learnt that the word she severed from the page was 'mamma', as in:

> …in the house in via Abate, at number two, *by a mother*
> who doesn't consent to be named, *was born a baby*
> of the female sex … [italics indicate the missing text]

I was now convinced of it. I felt it too, that her mother had renounced all of us, the descendants who came after. It was a kind of inherited rage. She had denied Natalina a mother, and us a deeper knowledge of ourselves.

One might have thought Natalina's mother's predicament – an unmarried mother, an illegitimate baby, nineteenth-century Roman Catholic Italy – would have elicited sympathy in me. After all, I was a mother myself. Who knew what oppressive social structures, what desperate personal circumstances, had confronted Natalina's mother.

I consider myself an empathetic person, one easily moved by vulnerability or injustice. As a teenager I wrote letters for Amnesty International campaigns demanding the release of political prisoners. As a journalist I so irritated a cabinet minister with my sympathetic newspaper articles about the plight of asylum seeker mothers of young children at the Villawood Immigration Detention Centre, he whispered, 'I am watching you' into the telephone. I despaired when the US Supreme Court overturned *Roe v Wade*. Cried when, the same year, my AFL club's women's team played their first ever match – because women weren't allowed to before. I consider myself progressive. A feminist.

Yet I judged her. *What kind of mother could forsake her child?* I asked. My discomfort only increased when I discovered Italy's foundling homes were known at the time as slaughterhouses for the number of babies who died there. Surely Natalina's mother knew this? Regardless, she put her baby there. And all the while she – the mother – still lived.

When I re-read those words, 'who does not consent to be named', I saw the midwife wrap the baby in hemp rags, close her black cloak around the child, lift her capacious bag of instruments from the floor. Wordlessly let herself out the front door of the damp and squalid house, clutching the wailing child to herself, like a thief with sacked jewels. I saw this woman, Rosa Rizzi, rush the newborn to the local parish priest to be secretly baptised before leaving for Bologna, because if there was one thing the Church would not stand for – as a Catholic I knew this much – it was the risk of a baby's soul being damned to spend eternity in hell. 'The child has no father,' I heard the midwife tell the cleric. 'The mother does not acknowledge her.' Then I saw them, midwife and baby, board the horse and carriage – the steam train was probably still too expensive for the peasant class – and make for the city gates.

At one year old, my son was not yet walking. It was 2012. We were in the master bedroom of our Canberra house. It was early evening, and the blinds were still open so that, through the large floor-to-ceiling windows, I could see the distant mountains and nature reserves to the northwest. Above a row of struggling lime trees, beyond the fence and neighbouring cottage, the tapered Telstra Tower across the other side of Lake Burley Griffin was lit up in neon.

My baby was nestled on the cushion of my wheelchair between my thighs. He faced outwards, towards the tower. I placed my hands gently beneath his armpits, lifted him up.

'Can you see it, darling?'

It was a ritual performance, something my baby and I shared. Every night, before Michael, my husband, put him to bed in his cot with sides too high for me to reach over from my wheelchair, we said goodnight to the luminous telecommunications tower.

The bedroom's timber floorboards were blond spotted gum that were starting to yellow with discoloration from the sun. The walls were white. To my left was a king-size bed and, above it, a large painting.

I couldn't decide whether I liked the painting or not. It was abstract and colourful but the colours were harsh, like bright city lights on a rainy day, with big, runny splotches of green, yellow, black, orange, purple and blue. In the bottom right-hand corner of the painting was a hot-pink splotch that, to my eye, looked like a woman. The figure was seated, but her legs were not really legs; they rose upwards instead of dropping down. In her lap was a small orange bundle which could almost, I thought, be a baby.

My son was getting heavier and it required effort to heave him up from my chair so that he could get the full view of the tower. I had done it many times before but this night I did it too quickly, gathered too much momentum. I was not holding him far enough in front to counterbalance my centre of gravity being weighted to the rear of the chair.

I felt the wheelchair tip backwards and suddenly we were flying through the air.

My baby. My baby.

My stomach whooshed, like I was on a sickening carnival ride. Flashes of window, painting, ceiling. It happened quickly but slowly; time was passing but was also suspended. Amid the stupefying terror came the thought: *Shield his head from the fall.*

I did it with my body, twisting and curling to my left so that, as we hit the floor, my shoulder slammed into the timber boards and his skull was, amazingly, spared any impact. Heart pounding, trembling, gasping, I held my baby, cradled him beside me on the floor. I could not believe what had just happened. My body ached in different places, but we were both intact.

Frantically, I called out to Michael in another room. I knew our son was unharmed, but I could not get us both back up onto the wheelchair without help. Also, I wanted a witness to the near catastrophe of my making, to my ineptitude as a mother.

Following this incident, my own mother tried to reassure me about my fitness for mothering. 'Don't you remember that when you were a baby, you fell off the change table when I wasn't looking?'

We all make mistakes, all us mothers, she was telling me. But I wasn't convinced. Motherhood, I thought, was more than I could handle. It was more than I deserved.

A line in a Sharon Olds poem makes me sit up straighter in my chair: 'the people who had hurt me most were my makers'.

I couldn't let it go. Not only the act of abandonment but my initial, aggrieved response to it. Something about what Natalina's mother did both compelled and horrified me. Was it because of how I was raised (in a 'traditional' two-parent family by a stay-at-home mother and a father in stable paid employment)? Or did it have something to do with my more recent history as a career-driven woman with latent aspirations of motherhood, surviving a terrible plane crash with devastating injuries and fearing I would never be able to have a child? Perhaps it was a combination of both things that meant I couldn't immediately grasp how a mother could forsake her child. It seemed extraordinary to me. Yet that mother and I were connected; we shared a common bloodline.

Impatient to understand her unimaginable deed, I threw out feelers for someone who could help me. First, I emailed an Italian genealogist and asked his advice about what was possible to learn in such cases. He wrote back that he could probably locate the record of her arrival at the 'orphanage', but that 'finding her parents will be 99.99% impossible'. He did not elaborate, and I sought no explanation for his extreme pessimism. Rather, I told myself that if it wasn't possible to know the particulars of Natalina's desertion, if her mother really was untraceable, then I would discover as much as I could about cases like hers.

For this I turned next to the daughter of an Italian friend who happened to be studying at the University of Bologna to ask if she would be interested in doing some research. I shared Natalina's birth document and told her about the *brefotrofio*. 'My poor great-grandmother wasn't even an orphan,' I wrote, 'she was an illegitimate or abandoned or endangered baby who lived not in an orphanage, but this institution called a *brefotrofio*. Have you ever heard of such a place?'

Milena accepted the assignment. From her initial investigations at the Biblioteca Salaborsa, Bologna's main public library, she identified the location of the *brefotrofio,* which appeared to have once been housed in the former convent of San Procolo. Most unexpectedly, she also tracked down the current whereabouts of its documents, which were held by the Archivio Storico Provinciale di Bologna.

It was more than I had hoped for, and my imagination fired. Were individual babies' files among the archived foundling home's documents? Was Natalina's?

Information continued to trickle in from Milena's exploration on the ground, and my own research on Google Scholar. Bologna's foundling home, I learnt, went by different names. More formally, it was known as l'Ospedale degli Esposti, 'the Hospital of the Exposed'. The word *esposti* referred to the way children were often abandoned: left in the open, in places of passage (on the doorsteps of houses, on church steps, at the edges of cultivated fields, on riverbanks, on rubbish heaps) so they would be found. More colloquially, it was known as l'Ospedale dei Bastardini, 'the Hospital of the Little Bastards'. Here were more words to make me flinch. I didn't like to think of any baby – let alone my own great-grandmother – as a bastard. I consulted a dictionary.

> Bastard, n. a person born of parents not married to each other; a child begotten and born out of lawful wedlock; an illegitimate child . . .

My great-grandmother's existence was unsanctioned, forbidden, because there was no man to take responsibility for her.

To understand why foundlings were treated differently to orphans (who were kept in separate institutions and given better living conditions), my researcher cautioned, I needed to appreciate the prominence of the Catholic Church in Italy, and how closely it was intertwined with the state. This was nowhere more so than in Bologna, a Papal State – under the direct rule of the pope – from the early 1500s until 1860, when it joined the newly formed secular Italian state, excluding a short period of Napoleonic rule. The Church distinguished between orphans whose next of kin, in the absence of their dead parents, were still officially responsible for them, and abandoned children. Because the latter were illegitimate, and their very existence involved a grave moral issue – the integrity of the 'traditional' family – they became the full responsibility of the state. They were also stigmatised and marginalised.

Keeping the abandoned babies in their care alive was only one of the foundling home's goals. The other was to protect the reputations of the unmarried pregnant women and their families from the shame of giving birth outside marriage. This was achieved by ensuring the abandoned child never discovered the identity of their mother. By concealing her name, the woman could one day marry and have a legitimate family. Once a woman 'chose' not to be named on her baby's birth records, her name was kept secret for one hundred years – like some fairytale enchantment. Midwives and foundling homes were sworn to secrecy. Women often gave birth in midwives' homes, so that their addresses were not discoverable from written records.

No wonder the genealogist had been so gloomy. Natalina was dead forty-two years by the time she had any right to begin looking for her mother. I agreed with him that – even though more than a century had passed – I would probably never find Natalina's mother.

For even greater anonymity, babies could be left at the *ruota degli esposti*, the foundling wheel, a rotating wooden cylinder connecting the foundling home to the street. Alerted to the arrival of the baby by a bell, a foundling home official on the other side would turn the wheel to collect the infant without seeing the person who had left it there. The wheels first appeared in the late Middle Ages to protect abandoned children from being eaten by animals, and later spread throughout Europe under Napoleon. In Naples, these wheels were believed to confer special blessings on babies. Sometimes when older children were being abandoned, their parents – wanting them to receive the Madonna's protection – smeared their oversized bodies with fats before squeezing them through the apertures, resulting in permanent injuries.

I pictured something like an after-hours library chute, an overflowing charity bin, the gaping mouth of a carnival clown. The idea of these contraptions chilled me. The hooded figure furtively thrusting a small bundle into the hollow in the wall then vanishing quietly into the night. The unseen hand slowly winding the squeaky, wooden wheel and the warm, fleshy, snuffling newborn materialising inside the hungry belly of the foundling home. It was a second birth, but the wheel-womb from which the child was reborn was cold and hard with no protective sac of temperature-controlled fluid, no placenta or umbilical cord supplying oxygen and nutrients. The wheel struck me as a potent symbol of the indifference with which I had imagined mothers regarded the babies they were abandoning.

Most northern Italian cities closed their wheels by 1875. This followed a movement led by progressive members of the Italian elite who argued the child abandonment system was out of control. Indeed, infant relinquishment was so common in the nineteenth century, the period became known as the century of foundlings. Reformers targeted foundling wheels for making it too easy for parents – especially married ones – to desert their children. I was disappointed when I learnt Bologna shut its foundling wheel in 1873, before Natalina's birth. It would have told me something more about her mother, if she had exploited such a convenience. So I thought.

I picked up the haunting black-and-white photograph of a young Natalina that had belonged to my nonna. My son called the era of black-and-white film 'in the grey time'. Natalina's dark features seemed exotic to me. Her bulbous black eyes and hair that was cut into a bob, elongating her nose and neck. Those eyes. Nonna had them too: the same round shape with sleepy lids. In Natalina's I read sadness and uncertainty. She wore a medallion that dangled above the curved neckline of her simple tunic. The longer I studied the image, the more details I noticed. The perfectly horizontal eyebrows. The crooked fringe. The stain on her sleeve. On the back of the photograph was scrawled: '*Riccordo Natalina Milocco – La mia mamma 1922 – Trieste*'. It was the year she left Bologna, the year before she ripped that birth certificate.

My vision at this stage was still binary. I saw only one victim, the hungry, wailing child, rejected at birth and stigmatised by Bolognese society. And then I saw the mother, denying her daughter her breast, refusing to acknowledge the child, withholding even her name, walking away.

It was 2007 when I emerged one day from a coma in an intensive care unit with my arms stretched out in a crucifix position, my body covered in bandages, not yet comprehending my injuries. I was thirty-four, a foreign affairs correspondent for a major newspaper. I had survived a plane crash.

When I was transferred to the burns unit, the treating surgeon who had removed my critically infected legs to save my life came to see me. One of the first questions I asked her – if not on that initial occasion, then one soon after – was: 'Will I be able to have children?' Not: will I be able to feed myself, sit up, walk, swim, write newspaper articles, watch football ever again (though they were all concerns). But will the burns on my abdomen, the infection that almost killed me, allow me to have a baby? And, further, was it permissible for me, whose body had been punished in this way – burned and flayed and shredded and cut and broken and sawn – to want this?

'I see no reason why not,' the doctor, who had six children of her own, replied.

When, some years later, I had not been able to fall pregnant, I met with a person who was familiar with the adoption process. It was an information-seeking exercise, one I approached as any woman who wished to be a mother and had not been able to have a child naturally might do. The person told me that I may not be able to adopt because some countries required mothers to have all their limbs, and I did not.

How their words stung; I feel their imprint still. Like a slap you were not expecting from a teacher across your arm from behind. How dare you. I had assumed that love, sense and good intentions were all a person needed to qualify them for parenthood. I didn't know there were people out there who thought me inadequately equipped to be a mother, because of my disability. Was it wrong of me to want a child? I no longer had my legs, but I still had my heart and brain. I found some kind medical professionals, was diagnosed with (and treated for) endometriosis and, with the aid of IVF, had my son.

I fought to have my child, never believing, until the moment the surgeon sliced open my belly on the operating table, that it would happen. I understood how lucky I was, knew that I would give my life for him in an instant. The maternal indifference I saw in Natalina's mother was beyond my experience, nothing I could conceive of.

One year after discovering the birth record, we unearthed Natalina's foundling home file. It transpired that it was indeed kept with all the other foundlings' files in the Archivio Storico Provinciale di Bologna.

It read like an impersonal journal of Natalina's life, from the moment the midwife carried her through the front doors, until the day she was married. There were records of the foundling home's payments to her country wet nurse. Payments to the foster parents with whom she was placed after being weaned. All her childhood illnesses and hospitalisations. The original letters she wrote to the foundling home after she became engaged. The discoveries were thrilling.

I thought about her mother, imagined her reading the file over my shoulder. Would she have been curious to know what was inside? Or would she have cringed to see the receipt the foundling home issued for the fee she paid to leave her daughter? Only half of it remained. Like a dry-cleaning docket, it was torn in two with the other part having gone with the midwife. Perhaps Natalina's mother would have preferred not to know the name and occupation of the woman at whose breast she fed for a year, nor of the husband and wife who taught Natalina her first words.

The mother would have also seen evidence of herself in the file. Not her name – that was secret, a detail not included in any foundling's records. But her tracks, like a hunted animal's. There was a browned page divided into three: questions, answers, observations. From this I learnt her address was the same as where Natalina was born: the house on Via Abate was evidently the mother's. The questions mainly concerned the mother's health, the birth, her gynaecological history. My skin prickled when I read her response to whether she'd had one or more miscarriages (*aborti*) or premature or stillbirths. 'Yes,' she had answered on the form.

Yes, there had been others? A female having that many pregnancies suggested she was older, not a girl herself. A single woman having that much sex in nineteenth-century Italy – what did that mean? My first thoughts were that she was either a prostitute or else someone was taking advantage of her. (A third possibility, that she was having lots of unmarried sex because she enjoyed it – perhaps she was in a relationship with a man she could not, or did not want to, marry – only occurred to me later.)

Unlike me, the midwife who had to convey the mother's answers to the doctors at the foundling home would have barely batted an eyelid at this revelation. She would have known all her secrets, I presumed; midwives usually did. But Natalina's mother had me worried now. Who was doing this to her?

As part of a strict Catholic upbringing, it was drilled into me that sex was a dangerous thing for a young, single woman, something to be feared. My mother was influenced by her authoritarian father, who warned if she fell pregnant before marrying never to darken his doorstep again. This was reinforced by the confessional. While dating my father, she felt compelled to confess at the end of every week to her local priest about their late-night 'parking' sessions (had she not confessed, she could not have taken Holy Communion on Sunday – so she believed). My father quipped that the priest must have looked forward to her visits.

My parents never threatened to disown me. They didn't have to. Boys were not allowed to telephone the house. A school-arranged pen pal in Year Nine once tried. The call was intercepted by my mother, and the boy was never heard from again. Caught in the bathroom with a safety razor and a foot on the sink, about to shave my legs for the first time aged fourteen or so, I was savaged. I can still see my mother's figure suddenly looming behind me in the mirror. My weakness in the face of peer pressure, she raged, would lead to heroin addiction (and, one might assume, teenage pregnancy).

My parents' attitudes, I suppose, were born out of fear for me, an impulse to protect. But it was as though I was being punished for growing up, for becoming a woman. Instead, my parents preferred to choose my partners for me. My mother arranged, without my consent, for the son of a local doctor to accompany me to my Year Ten formal.

Later, when I was at university, she prayed to the Holy Spirit that a medical student who was the son of a friend of hers from church would ask me out. 'It worked – I couldn't believe it – but you hated it.' To this day she doesn't understand why her actions so offended me.

These things stay with you.

At seventeen, I was as obsessed with boys as the rest of my all-girls Catholic high school cohort, but I kept them at a distance. I finished high school and enrolled in a law degree. Early motherhood was inconceivable to me, an end to life as I knew it. Through my university years I had a mantra that I repeated often, as letters I wrote to a friend in Melbourne attest: 'I will always be free and keep myself whole.' Today I am unsure what I meant by that, but reading those letters it is clear I feared that my liberty, my independence, could be taken away if I did not continually reassert and protect them. By my mid-twenties, when plenty of my friends were getting engaged, I wrote that: 'Marriage is definitely not on my agenda, I think it is such an unnecessary extravagance.'

I was so late finding a serious boyfriend (not until my thirties) that cousins on my father's side decided I was gay. In my letters to that same friend, I pondered whether God wanted me to join the convent, then lamented that: 'I don't think there's any chance of it happening. I'm too gutless, too weak to do something like that.'

Did this personal history explain my somewhat aghast response to Natalina's mother's multiple pregnancies? Did it reflect a long-suppressed fear that began with the Church and was conditioned in my mother and then in me? And what was the fear of exactly? What was so frightening about women like her?

The more I learnt about Natalina's birth, the greater my fixation with her mother grew – to the bemusement, sometimes irritation, of my family.

Despite sharing my early finding that Natalina was a foundling, my mother continued to insist she was an orphan.

'No, she wasn't,' I said. 'She had parents. She had a mother.'

To prove it, I went and got a dictionary.

'See,' I said. '"Orphan, noun. A child whose father and mother are dead."'

I kept hoping my mother would remember some new detail about Natalina that she hadn't told me before, something about her early life in Bologna. When I pressed her, though, she grew frustrated. I needed to appreciate that in the aftermath of World War II nobody had the time or inclination to interrogate grandparents about their childhoods.

One night we were at dinner at my parents' house when I decided to share some of my recent archival findings on Natalina with the wider family. I assumed, incorrectly, that everybody else would be as interested as I was.

'Where are you finding this rubbish?' cried my mother. 'Oh, if your nonno heard you.'

'What other bombshells have you got for us?' Michael joked.

When I continued, undeterred, explaining how Natalina was lucky to have survived the foundling home, which – I had discovered – was ravaged at the time of her birth by syphilis, my brother giggled.

'Now you are going to say we were responsible for bringing syphilis to Australia.'

When I then announced I was planning a research trip to Bologna, my mother and sister both called me 'crazy'. (To be honest, I secretly wondered if I was too; we had only just moved from Canberra to Sydney.)

Months later, I telephoned my mother to relay yet another new discovery, and in a tone of exasperation she cut me off.

'But everyone's dead,' she said.

It was as though all the people for whom it was reasonable to have cared about Natalina and her birth story were gone. And that it was an affront for me, because of the generations that lay between us, to care so much.

But I did care. I was drawn to the stories of those who came before. It mattered to me to find the mother. I was a journalist, a truth seeker. I was also struggling to make sense of my own life's bewildering course. Unfortunately, this urge to dig deeper, to make myself vulnerable in the pursuit of connection, made me an outlier in our family, especially among the women.

Sometimes I pondered whether life wouldn't be easier if it were otherwise. When a poem landed in my inbox one day, 'Our Dust' by C.D. Wright, I thought perhaps the universe was telling me that yes, it would be preferable if I let the past be.

I am your ancestor. You know next-to-nothing
about me.
There is no reason for you to imagine
the rooms I occupied or my heavy hair.

'No reason'. And yet I perceived a contradiction in this poem. The word 'heavy' implied a weight that carried forward, even after death. A weight that reverberated, that didn't want to be ignored.

I was excavating my maternal line. I was doing it for Natalina, a woman I had never met, who was forever denied a mother's love. And I was doing it for those in my family who the mother sought to sever herself from: my grandmother, my mother and me.

Only afterwards did a potential explanation for the resistance I was experiencing around my research occur to me. 'Inheritances,' writes American scholar Saidiya Hartman, 'are chosen as much as they are passed on.' I was disrupting a more comfortable family narrative. One that, quite possibly, had been deliberately created.

It continued to trouble me, how swiftly I had judged the mother. Was it because of my insecurity about my own mothering? That sense of inadequacy, that fear of doing harm?

I was nervous holding my baby and never did it while walking on prosthetic limbs. I didn't trust my broken body not to hurt him. Michael did much of L's early caring, especially anything that involved carrying him – activities I always associated intrinsically with motherhood as I had experienced it as a child. Simple things, like pushing his pram to our local park or, when he'd learnt to walk, holding his hand to cross the road.

Making dinner in the kitchen or working in my study, I'd picture the two of them out walking the dog. My son would be strapped into a backpack-style baby carrier on his father's back. They would follow the stony ridge at the end of our street. Beneath the canopy of yellow box and red gum, Michael would point out the snowy Brindabellas in the distance. At a certain point he would set down L, who would kick up the leaves with his wobbly legs. Michael sometimes took photos so I could see where they had been, what adventures they'd had.

I often felt guilty that my son was missing out in different ways because I was not an able-bodied mother. If those adoption gatekeepers were right, that I was unfit to be a mother of an adopted child, did it not follow that I would let down a biological one too? There were many practical things I could still do for my boy, I reminded myself – dressing and feeding him, booking his appointments, reading with him – at least I had these. I was deeply conscious of how great a privilege it was to mother this beautiful boy, to love and to be loved by him. My very own, much-wanted son. Yet the misgivings continued to plague me. That, having given birth to my son, I wasn't good enough, whole enough, worthy of being his mother.

It seemed I was as agonised by my judgement of Natalina's mother, by my moral outrage over something that occurred more than a century ago, as I was by my incessant judging of my own mothering because of something bad that had happened to me, through no fault of my own. I became aware of my prejudices around motherhood, ones I didn't know I had. That urge to hold the mother accountable for all ills. I thought of the ways I felt judged and judged myself as a mother. For wanting a child as a disabled mother. For being an older mother. For using IVF. For bottle-feeding from six weeks because the burns made breastfeeding too painful. For having an only child and not trying harder for a sibling, because birthing for me was deemed high risk and we didn't want to push our luck. For bringing to motherhood some of the trauma of what had happened to me.

There is a diary entry from around the time I found Natalina's birth record. L was five:

> I'm going along OK, then it's like I can't take it anymore, this life in a fucking wheelchair pushing myself between walls to move, putting things on my lap to carry them – motherhood domestic things – and they slide off and I just want to scream but I don't … I try to be positive, I try not to let L see my rage but sometimes I can't pretend, I can't hold it all in.

I began to see, as I couldn't at first, how Natalina's mother and I were both mothers with constraints that placed us outside the social norm. I desperately wanted to be a 'total' mother to my son but could not. Was it the same for her? Perhaps I needed to find her because if I could understand what had caused her to give up her child, I would not have to think of her, my ancestor, as a bad mother. And if I could forgive her, maybe I could forgive myself.

Thus far, however, I knew little about Natalina's mother's personal circumstances. Was it possible to know more? It was suggested I try the parish where Natalina was baptised. The baptismal archives of the Collegiate Church of San Giovanni Battista went back 500 years. Volunteers commenced a search, based on Natalina's date of birth.

At my desk in Sydney, I waited. Was the mother hidden in there, somewhere? I felt as an archaeologist must, having stumbled upon the location of an ancient burial ground. This archaeological site belonged to my family, and I couldn't wait to dig it up. It didn't occur to me that I might unearth things that were best left in the ground.

2
Margins

Imagine this. You cannot walk your child to the school gate, so you miss those early interactions with other mothers at drop-off and pick-up from which new bonds with other families take root. Your husband, who takes your child to school, sees how sad this makes you. He keeps an eye out for mothers he thinks you might like and returns home excitedly waving his iPhone, where he has stored their names and phone numbers for you. He has told these other mothers about you, and now you can invite them for playdates at your house and get to know them over mugs of peppermint tea while the children muck about in the garden.

You cannot be a 'tuckshop mum' like your own mother was. You won't ever make scores of Devon and tomato sauce sandwiches in one morning and place them inside brown paper bags marked with the names of other people's children. And you won't get to wave to your child at lunchtime when they come out of class or tell the other mothers working beside you, 'See, that's my child there.' But you hear that the teachers need volunteers to read with the children, so you sign up for that and your husband takes you and it is wonderful, being in the classroom with your child, getting to know their classmates, their daily routine. There is a curious thrill in being seen by the other children as a mother, as though you need the affirmation of random five-year-olds.

You cannot volunteer to marshal at athletics carnivals, nor can you offer to accompany your child's class on school excursions. But you see the Parents and Friends association needs representatives for the upcoming school year and, after confirming that much of it can be done online, you put up your hand and a kind mother – over time you meet many – agrees to share the position with you. This way she can perform any tasks that require you to be physically present in ways you cannot be. As a bonus in this role, you can push for more thought to be given to making social events physically accessible to everyone.

(This follows some disheartening experiences. The class rep who decides to break with her counterparts in the other kindergarten classes arranging get-to-know-you events for the mothers. Instead of a dinner, your class rep organises a bushwalk up Canberra's Red Hill. Or the sporting-club parent another year who tells you sure, they can move the end-of-season drinks to the downstairs part of the pub with no lift. But only if you can assure them you're coming, because it is nicer upstairs.)

Try as you do, however, even when it is you who organises the event, at a location without stairs, you can still find yourself, a mother with disability, on the periphery. You cannot easily mingle, move from one group to the next. You need to sit down, but not on those tall stools – that won't work for someone whose leg is held on with a metal pin. You end up marooned on a low chair pushed against some wall or tree, unable to smoothly get up and leave when the conversation becomes tired. You feel yourself becoming an awkward burden to whomever you are talking to, so you release them. 'Feel free to go and talk to the others,' you say. 'No really,' you insist. 'I will be fine.' Now you are alone, nursing your glass of unpleasantly warm white wine. Around you the noisy crush of bodies continues with its urgent socialising, like a frenzied colony of insects. You watch the women in high heels enviously: how carefree they seem. Perhaps one of them will notice you and pull up a chair.

Disability places you outside the mothering mainstream and because of this it makes your family, in some ways, outsiders too. It can be exhausting, constantly fighting against marginalisation, trying to convince others and yourself that you have just as much right as anyone to be a mother.

Maybe this is why I was so intent upon the trip to Bologna. Of course, it was about uncovering a long-kept family secret, trying to answer that question of why my great-grandmother was abandoned. But truth be told, it was also about creating an 'experience' for my family. This was my version of motherhood, where I tried to compensate for the fact that – because of my injuries, my disabilities – our son often misses out on things other 'normal' families get to do. When a former colleague cautioned that the cobblestones would make travelling in Italy too difficult for someone in a wheelchair (as if I didn't know), I didn't listen, just barrelled ahead.

I picture the holidays of my childhood. Our big orange tent with the sticky zipper and a large plastic window, which heated up the annexe beside the sleeping compartment like a greenhouse. Furniture my father made from parts scrounged at the tips where he worked as a surveyor: shelves fashioned out of wooden ironing boards, broken stools tied together with rope. The campsite cluttered with snorkels and buckets and floaties and wet towels and cans of Aerogard. The noisy chorus of cicadas, the fragrant scent of eucalyptus. My sister and I in crochet bikinis, our hair Medusa-like, damp and matted from carefree days spent swimming in the lake with sea lice that made us itch. Feet encrusted with black sand. Afternoons swatting march flies and their stinging bites. Covering my brother's sunburnt back with gum leaves, the two of us laughing raucously. My mother carting water from one side of the campsite to the other, because my father insisted on pitching our tent as far away as possible from the other campers. Frying up tinned spam on a kerosene stove.

Today's typical middle-class Australian family holidays are more likely to be had in (inaccessible) Airbnbs shared with friends, or child-friendly resorts in tropical Fiji or Bali. None of it, certainly not the camping, was practical for a mother with two prosthetic limbs.

And so there we sat in the Sydney spring of 2018 on an A380, being buffeted by unseasonably hot, gusting winds that were preventing us from taking off. Inside, the plane's cabin was warm and airless. I would rather have been anywhere than stranded on the tarmac, except in the air. Every fibre of my being screamed: *why have you brought us here?* The muscles, neurons, proteins remembered and demanded an explanation for this insanity. I ordered myself not to lose it. *You are a mother.*

Beside me was our son, six years old, blond hair snipped into a crew cut, wearing an aquamarine t-shirt with a shark on the front; his favourite animal, he claimed. He was eating Skittles and playing on his iPad, and I let him, even though it was almost midnight. On his other side, across the aisle, sat my husband. 'Are you okay?' he mouthed, and I shrugged my shoulders. I felt safer knowing Michael was with us, that much I knew. His presence, his willingness to support my lofty schemes, made such an ambitious trip possible.

My limbs throbbed. I wanted to remove the prosthetics but couldn't yet in case we missed the airport curfew and had to disembark suddenly. I worried about how I would store them when we did take off, in the limited space between my seat and the row in front, so that other passengers didn't see them, and decided I would cover them with my jacket. I hated that I cared so much about this, what other people thought. It felt weak, pathetic, when it was my job to be strong for my son.

I pulled out the still-pristine copy of the *Bologna Pocket Guide* I had purchased online some months ago, turned to the page about children and found, to my dismay, a sad and solitary paragraph that began: 'Bologna is not the obvious choice for children, especially given the sparsity of parks and gardens in the centre.' I regretted not reading the guide before now, but not my decision to uproot our lives and give this a go. There were good reasons, I told myself, for putting us through this. For pulling our son out of school for a term. For the three of us taking Italian lessons for the past year. And for why we were now going to spend the European winter in a medieval city that was, apparently, not fit for children.

The plane was cleared to depart, and we were airborne. I pulled a scratchy grey airline blanket over L, and he drifted off to sleep. Michael settled in to watch a Bollywood movie. Discreetly as possible I removed the prosthetics, resting them in the space between our son and me, shielding them from view with spare clothing. Then, reluctantly, I swallowed the Valium I had brought along just in case and mumbled a prayer to 'please let it work'.

Two weeks before departing for Bologna, I was sitting at my computer one night. I was making final preparations for our trip, probably getting last-minute instructions from our son's teachers for the home-schooling I had naïvely promised to do, when an email arrived.

'I have some really great news: I think we have found the name of Natalina's mother.'

Heart and breath halted in that pregnant moment. I read on. The mother's name was Ersilia Serra.

Seeing the name for the first time, I brimmed with an excitement I knew was unshared with anyone living. I wanted to call out to the universe (to the spirit-verse) so my great-grandmother could hear: 'I have found your mother.'

I could not see her face, but I had a name. A name! I had never believed it possible, had never dreamt there was even a remote prospect I would uncover it. But it turned out the mother was there all along, waiting for me in the parish archives. Given a 0.01 per cent chance, I had found her.

Volunteers working in the San Giovanni Battista parish archives had located her name in a clandestine book where the baptisms of all the town's illegitimate babies were recorded, going back to 1566. The book was titled, in the original Latin, *Liber in quo Baptismata Secreta Describuntur*; in English, this loosely translates to 'The Book of Secret Baptisms'.

It sounded, again, like something out of a fairytale. Who knew such a book existed? My first response was to ask my researcher, 'What is a secret baptism?' So little did I understand, still, of the role of the

Catholic Church in the lives of illegitimate children and their mothers. All I could think, back then, was that every family has its secrets, but one did not expect to find them in a book labelled as such.

A picture formed in my mind of what this tome would look like: the colour of molasses, unmarked, bulging with the names of illegitimate babies. I assumed it would have been concealed in its day, perhaps inside a locked drawer or a hidden chamber beneath some stairs.

When I eventually held the volume in my hands, in a meeting room behind the San Giovanni Battista church, it was nothing of the kind. Small and thin, it had a cracked and wrinkled grey-and-flesh-coloured cover with the title on the front. On its spine was written *Battesimi segreti 1803–1903*. It was a ghost of a book, not bloated at all. Nor was it secreted away. Sometimes the babies whose baptisms were recorded inside were born out of wedlock, but their parents later married; in these cases, the baby's name would be scrubbed from the secret book and admitted into the official parish register.

Natalina was the fourteenth baby to be covertly baptised in San Giovanni in Persiceto that year. This is a translation of what the priest wrote, in sloping cursive, beside a narrow column with a number and the baby's made-up surname (Mirci):

> On the twenty-third of December 1898 I, the undersigned chaplain curate, baptised a young girl, daughter of an unknown father (and of Ersilia Serra), born on the twenty-third of December 1898 at 9.30am in S. Giovanni in Persiceto via Abate n.2, who was given the names Natalina Lea Maria and the surname Mirci. Godmother Rizzi Rosa in Scagliarini. She was presented by Rizzi Rosa in Scagliarini, public midwife, who declared the above. In faith, Don Barbieri Giuseppe chaplain.

Here were the Church's tentacles again, inking these women and their babies, casting them out to the margins of society. Maintaining its grip by imposing mandatory rituals on its unfortunate subjects, then forcing them underground. The priest's entry was a secret pact with God to save my great-grandmother's soul.

The significance of the name. Mirci, the surname given to Ersilia's baby, bore no connection to San Giovanni or its inhabitants. Unlike Serra, which was a typical last name of the town – and could, one day, give the child a clue to her background – Mirci had never been recorded by the office of the *anagrafe* (civil registry) of the San Giovanni municipality before. It was probably chosen by Rosa Rizzi. Had it been the Bastardini hospital's choice, she would have been named after a mineral, plant or animal. This foundling home convention emerged after the circulars of 1811, which set down new rules for naming abandoned babies.

Before this, surnames were chosen that served as lifelong reminders of the children's foundling origins. Names such as Gettatelli ('Thrown away'), Spurio ('Spurious'), Incertopadre ('Uncertain Father') and Lasciati ('Left'). Different cities' foundling homes had their preferred appellations. In Bologna it was *Degli Esposti* ('Of the Exposed'); in Florence it was *Innocenti* ('Innocents'); in Milan *Colombo* ('Dove'); in Siena *Della Scala* ('Of the Step', a common place babies were left). Eventually such practices were banned for being confusing and cruel, although their legacy lives on through some of Italy's most common surnames today. Someone with the surname 'Esposito', for instance, can be almost certain of the existence of a foundling ancestor.

Giving Natalina a name with no connection to any person or town marked the child in other ways. She was untethered not only from her family and genetic history, but from her community, her village. She would always feel displaced. No inherited town customs (San Giovanni was famous for its hemp processing); no connection to the geography of the fertile plains, given over to agriculture since the swampland was reclaimed for farming in the ninth century. She became a permanent outsider, existing in the margins of society. For so long as she carried that made-up surname, Mirci, she belonged to the *pio luogo*, the 'pious place', the foundling home: this was her only identity. She was forever a *figlia del luogo*, a 'daughter of the place'.

It felt like a minor miracle, unearthing the mother's name when foundling homes took such care to prevent that ever happening – and it was. When I checked with archivists in Bologna, they confirmed that finding the name of the mother in cases of nineteenth-century child abandonment was '*quasi impossibile*'. It remains the law in Italy today that the mother's name must be kept secret for 100 years from a baby she chooses to relinquish. This concealment is thought to discourage abortion.

Today proper records are kept so that, should a child ever want to know their mother, the Carabinieri can locate her to ascertain whether, with the passage of years, she consents to this happening. In Ersilia's time, however, no such records were kept and finding the mother's name was a matter of luck. Sometimes parish records contained information about the mother because priests had more freedom than foundling hospitals when it came to recording baptisms of abandoned children. It was such a priest, the independently minded Don Giuseppe Barbieri, who transcribed Ersilia's name into 'The Book of Secret Baptisms'.

I should not have been so surprised by the existence of this book. But then, I do not recall the Counter-Reformation's implications for women's rights ever being a part of the religious education curriculum in my twelve years of Catholic schooling. Historian David Kertzer writes that when the Catholic Church's power was challenged by Protestantism, it reacted by aggressively asserting its authority over women's reproductive freedoms. Before then, there was no clear distinction between a legitimate and an illegitimate child; the definition of marriage was ambiguous, and priests did not have a significant role in officiating over what constituted an acceptable partnership and family. From the sixteenth century onwards, however, only the Church could decide which sexual relations were lawful: namely, those sanctioned by a priest through the sacrament of marriage. Illegitimate pregnancies were abhorrent, with the stigma attaching to the women. To prevent women whose honour was at stake from resorting to infanticide and abortion, the Church sanctioned anonymous abandonment, with priests encouraging mothers to relinquish their babies to the foundling home.

Foundling homes are said to date back to the twelfth-century Pope Innocent III, who was moved by fishermen's reports of dead babies in the River Tiber to establish the first one. These institutions then proliferated throughout Catholic Europe in the seventeenth and eighteenth centuries. By the nineteenth century, foundling homes were overwhelmed. In some Italian cities, a third of all babies were being abandoned; in Bologna, it was a fifth. This might seem contradictory in a culture where family is celebrated and mothers are venerated. But there was a combination of reasons for this phenomenon: industrialisation, population growth, more women undertaking paid work. Underpinning it all was the influence of the Catholic Church.

Why did Don Barbieri include Ersilia's name in the secret book when her anonymity was mandated by the foundling home's rules, in accordance with the Church's position? Was the priest a fastidious record keeper? Moved with compassion for the child who might one day come searching? Or did this act of recording Ersilia's name connect her to her 'sin'? Whatever his motivations, this much is undeniable. If it weren't for that secret book, I would not have found Ersilia. It was the critical trace she unknowingly left, an earthly cord connecting her to her daughter, and to those of us who came after. What did it mean that her name had been discovered after all this time? And that I was the person who found it?

Learning Ersilia's name back in Sydney, I scrounged for a connection to our family. There were no other Ersilias among us, but the name of the great-aunt in whose possession Natalina's birth record remained all the years since her death also began with an E and had the same number of letters. Etuilla was my nonna Anna's capricious youngest sister. She was childless, and not by choice; she tried many times to become a mother, and it was painful for her that her attempts never succeeded. (When my mother was primary school-aged, she remembers being bundled into their small car with her parents and sister and being forced to sit between Etuilla's knees. 'Don't press your aunt's stomach,' she was told, cryptically.)

This was, admittedly, a tenuous connection. I was looking, I suppose, for proof that more powerful and mysterious forces were at play than just the ones we mortals could easily explain, like genetic inheritance. Why was it so important to know this, the significance of Ersilia's name? What's in a name? Does it tell us something about the person, or just those who chose the name, what mattered to them? My mother named me for a June Allyson character in a movie she liked as a child, aptly called *Too Young to Kiss*. It's a name that has never fitted me, one I have never grown into. She named my younger brother, her first-born son, for her maternal grandfather, Natalina's husband from Trieste, Antonio Milocco. A man who defied his family's wishes by marrying a foundling.

In Roman mythology, Hersilia was a Sabine woman from the central Apennine Mountains (the range that separates Bologna from Florence to the south) who married Romulus, the founder and first king of Rome. Hersilia is credited with ending the war between Rome and the Sabine people, whose women the Romans abducted to forcibly populate their city. The episode is known as 'The Rape of the Sabines'. I doubt Ersilia's parents had in mind this story of exploited women, violence against women and forced pregnancies when they chose this name for her.

'Ersilia.' I played with the pronunciation, tried rolling the 'r', but found the 's' sound afterwards made it difficult. It tripped my tongue.

I had planned the Bologna trip assuming I would never know who the mother was. Suddenly, my delvings in that city took on a whole new purpose. With a name I could learn about Ersilia's family, events in her life and hopefully – if it was still knowable, 120 years later – come closer to understanding her seemingly incomprehensible act.

After that initial exhilarating revelation of Ersilia's name, information had continued to dribble in from the other side of the world. Some of the details were messy, disturbing, and I had put off thinking about them too much. Arriving in Bologna, I could no longer delay confronting the contents of emails from the San Giovanni volunteers.

As I had suspected, Ersilia was not a young woman when she gave up her daughter. She was thirty-three and unmarried and would remain single all her life. Much more shocking to me – the revelation that punctured my elation at discovering her hidden identity – was this. When her daughter was born, Ersilia already had a son, a seven-year-old named Paolino, whom she had kept, and whose father was *ignoto*, unknown, too.

Why would she have kept a son but not a daughter? She clearly found a way to keep one child; why could she not have kept two?

To my researcher I wrote: 'That is very interesting indeed – first the name, Ersilia, and now this. I don't know what to make of it. Why would she have kept her son and not her daughter (maybe a son was valued more?). I wonder what profession Ersilia was – a domestic, something else? It is very mysterious and not at all what I expected.'

In my journal I was more candid – and prudish: 'I don't know what to think. I went from thinking she just abandoned her child to thinking how judgemental I had been, when she was probably forced into it. To finding out she had a child already and kept him. What was she – a prostitute? Do I want to know any more? This is such a strange story, who was this woman, my forebear. I don't just come from peasants; I come from prostitutes. Goodness gracious.'

In many of the cases I had come across through my reading, mothers who abandoned an illegitimate child tended to marry eventually and then have legitimate children. Yet Ersilia didn't do this. She kept her illegitimate firstborn child, knowing the social repercussions – that it virtually guaranteed she would not marry (placing her among a minority 6 per cent of San Giovanni women) and would remain ostracised from society. Why? Was it because a boy could provide for her one day? Or something else?

Attitudes towards legitimacy and abandonment started to change following Italian unification in the 1860s, and the moral stranglehold of the Church waned in the final decades of the nineteenth century. However, as the Bologna archivists confirmed, in Italian society up until the 1960s a woman pregnant out of wedlock was considered 'a marked woman for life'. This was particularly so in a small town like San Giovanni and in a former Papal State like Bologna. Such a woman, they told me, was 'a body anyone could use'.

Ersilia the outcast I could well imagine. Perhaps neighbours ignored her in the shops; maybe the priest refused her entry into his church. But Ersilia the 'body anyone could use'? Was this for sex? I tried to conjure what the phrase meant, in flesh-and-blood terms. Men assuming that they could possess her body at any time; her community condoning this because fallen women needed to be punished for their sins, for having bad morals, for sexual promiscuity. What were we talking about here, exactly? Violent rape? Or something less brutal? How did Ersilia see herself? Did she believe her body no longer belonged to her?

All this ruminating led me to wonder what Ersilia and I had in common. Shame was something I knew about. During my son's infancy I rarely allowed Michael to photograph the two of us together. I took photos of my son with his full-bodied father instead. As the memories of that time fade, I find myself a phantom mother in my son's early years, absent from the photographic record.

I do not feel ashamed of my body with people who know me well. I feel it with people who do not: the random delivery guy who comes to the door and asks what happened to me. The parent of my son's friend, whom I have never met before, who stops by our house to pick up their child after a playdate, the stare that lingers too long on the spaces where my legs used to be. I fear how these strangers view me, that they see me only as a freakish body to be ogled, pitied, interrogated, talked about behind my back. I have always disliked certain things about my appearance. As a child I used to pray at mass on Sundays for God to give me more slender hands. Now there is so much more I want to hide.

But the shame wasn't only over my physical difference; it was also over my deficiencies as a mother. I could never be as active and present a mother in my son's life as other mothers – those we encountered at school, around sports teams – and sometimes, because of this, I didn't want to be seen at all.

Did Ersilia and I share shame in ceding power to others to define us? Perhaps here lay the difference between our shames. Ersilia's was imposed by society on all women in her position. Mine is more internalised. Why it matters so much to be reminded of my difference, I struggle to explain. But I keep trying to in the hope that if, one day, I do understand my shame, I will not have to feel it anymore.

My questions for Ersilia were piling up. If Natalina was her second child, who were these children's fathers? Was it the same man? What kind of situation was she in where she could have two illegitimate babies, not to mention those miscarriages?

The sorry fact is the existence of a prior illegitimate child was not the most disturbing detail to materialise in those emails. There was also this: in that house on Via Abate, Ersilia and her son lived with her father, Teodoro – a widower.

The image of Ersilia in that cramped apartment after the midwife whisked baby Natalina away was morphing, taking on new characters, new undertones. I now saw her stirring a thin cabbage *minestra* in a large copper cauldron, the same one in which she'd just boiled the bloody birth rags. I pictured two figures who were watching on hungrily, waiting for their dinner: a small, confused boy who had just witnessed his mother giving birth to a baby sister, who was then taken away by a woman with a big black bag; and a sullen-faced old man who had a daughter for a wife.

My mind went to dark places. The story was messy, strange, and didn't fit with others I had read about. As terrible as those other stories were, Ersilia's hinted at something different that I could not yet articulate. I wondered when Ersilia's mother had died. I hoped it was after Paolino was born. I didn't mention this new detail to Michael, with whom I shared all my research. Was I in denial? This was my bloodline.

The volunteers from San Giovanni, when I questioned them, thought Ersilia gave away her child because of poverty. This group of women, whom I would later meet in person, were experts in secret baptisms.

Ersilia's father, they told me, was a *canapino*, a hemp worker, a physically arduous job he could not have continued into old age. He was sixty-three when Natalina was born. Ersilia, they confirmed, was a domestic servant, not a prostitute. This was probably why the family moved to the town from San Giacomo del Martignone in the countryside, where she was born, so she could find employment to support him. Her pregnancy likely happened in the house where she worked – an all-too-common story at the time. Ersilia was a single mother, sustaining two others on her salary, responsible for all household tasks – the cooking, cleaning, washing – and without prospects for improving her situation. Her desperation and powerlessness when she fell pregnant a second time were obvious. In the words of one of the San Giovanni women, 'Ersilia wanted to cut her ties with the second child because she already had her hands full with one.'

I wanted to believe the poverty, hands-too-full theory. Ersilia was born in 1865. Her early adulthood, when she gave birth to Paolino, was a period of severe economic crisis in Italy caused by international factors affecting agriculture. Impoverishment was widespread. The idea, for example, that she was too poor to feed a second child was palatable to me. Life was difficult. Peasants at that time lived on saltless corn-based polenta, temporarily filling but so devoid of nutrition that eating it and nothing else was like consuming small doses of poison.

(This polenta disease has a name, pellagra. It is caused by a deficiency of vitamin B3, niacin, and results from eating only maize flour. Its symptoms include a rash that forms around the neck like a scaly, red necklace and it can eventually lead to delirium and dementia.)

I could accept the idea that Ersilia, having to work to feed her young son and enfeebled father, was impregnated by a predatory boss. Perhaps she had no means to amass even the smallest of dowries to attract a husband, and this was why she remained single. She was condemned to enduring unwanted pregnancies by poverty and religion (no different to women in places where abortion is banned today, such as in Trump's America).

Yet some details of Ersilia's story didn't align with the poverty theory. How, for example, did she afford the twenty-lire fee for the foundling home, plus the midwife's transportation costs?

Then the San Giovanni women went and found Paolino's baptismal record. It was in 'The Book of Secret Baptisms' too:

> On May 23, 1891, I the undersigned, baptised a newborn son of an unknown father and Ersilia Serra, daughter of Teodoro and the late Enrica Fabbri, born on May 21, 1891 at 01:00 a.m. in the Parish of San Giovanni Battista in Persiceto, Via Umberto 1 No 39, whose name was Paolino Amedeo Maria (surname) Serra. Godmother Rosa Manganelli was presented the child by public midwife Rosa Rizzi in Scagliarini. In faith, Don Pier Giovanni C. Manganelli, Chaplain and Curate.

There was the midwife, Rosa Rizzi, once again hovering around the edges of Ersilia's reproductive life, privy to all her secrets. This time, however, a woman other than Rosa was the baby's godmother. This was possible because Ersilia had accepted Paolino; she had given him her surname.

And there also was Enrica Fabbri, Ersilia's late mother. Already dead by the time Ersilia gave birth to Paolino. This was not the result I had been hoping for. I would have preferred Ersilia was a prostitute. Then I would still not have known who her children's father was – but at least it was less likely to have been Teodoro.

It was a disruptive act, this dredging up of a hidden ancestor. Like locating a long-lost shipwreck in the dark and frigid ocean depths, not knowing what relics it might contain. Hoping for treasures but retrieving cargo of a different kind: a bloated body whose skin has peeled away, its flesh nibbled by crabs and fish. A crate of sodden dynamite. From it, piecing together a story that was never intended to be told.

I knew how easily a life could be undone. The death of the mother. The work trip you wish you'd never gone on. What I hadn't expected was that putting a life back together again – one that had been lost to time and existed only in fragments – could also be disruptive. Disruptive to the ideas and images you have about yourself and your family, about where you came from and what made you.

Following that discovery of the widowed father, I gave voice to my secret fears in my journal. 'What if the father was her father too and I am the result of some incestuous relationship? I don't know if I want to know any more.'

But it was too late. Having found the mother, I could not now unknow her. I had forced back together the ties she had so determinedly ruptured between our lives – hers with those of her daughter and her descendants – and I could not go and break them again.

Saidiya Hartman uses the phrase 'writing at the limit of the unspeakable and the unknown' to describe her work of bringing to life the stories of African women imprisoned on slave ships. Hartman, a descendant of slaves, grapples with the ethics of representing the interior lives of these women whose existences she uncovered in the archives of Atlantic slavery. So little can be known of them – their voices having been muted in the archives by slave traders. But not trying means upholding that very same silence.

Hartman's conception gave me a new way to view my own foray into the archives. I felt myself in a similar place in my excavations into Ersilia's life, teetering 'at the limit of the unspeakable and the unknown', uncertain as to how – and whether – to go on.

Until now, our family had lived unbounded lives, in complete ignorance of this woman's existence. And I had gone and undone that. There was, I realised, not only work in uncovering the past; there was also work in knowing it.

We arrived in Bologna on a cloudy Sunday afternoon and went straight to our lodgings. After our landlady left, we fell asleep for a few hours, waking in time for dinner. It was cold outside, the air was damp, and my son cried protest tears at being forced out into the creepy night. But I was impatient for signs of Ersilia and wanted to explore immediately. Plus, we needed to eat.

One of the city's nicknames is La Rossa, 'the red one', for its ubiquitous red bricks, wavy red roof tiles, red external window coverings. The city is red by day, but not by night. Bologna after dark is eerie yellow. Yellow as in *giallo*, the name given to Italian crime novels. Yellow as in the colour of a jaundiced newborn. Yellow, the colour of mourning and betrayal. The xanthous glow was emitted by lanterns that dangled beneath the medieval porticoes. It swirled around us like a sinister fog that first evening, when we emerged jet-lagged onto Via Parigi, our crooked street, searching for a meal.

Halfway along the peculiarly shaped street we reached the site of a deconsecrated seventh-century church, San Colombano. It protruded at an odd angle, pinching the street in two like an hourglass. Homeless people slept under the raised portico out the front, against a backdrop of patchy frescoes.

We skirted around the ancient building, Michael helping me by pushing my wheelchair along the bumpy cobblestoned road until we could return to the smooth paths beneath the more accessible porticoes. Here, where the street narrowed, sounds reverberated off the brick buildings either side, like we were passing through a timeless urban canyon. I imagined the horses and carriages that would have clopped and creaked and jingled along the confined laneways; the street vendors who would have obstructed their easy passage with woven baskets of different wares; the air that would have been pungent with manure, urine, and smoke from the constant burning of woodfires.

We turned the corner onto Via Galleria – once the city's most noble street, full of aristocratic mansions – and it was then that I saw them. The winged infant babies, the *putti*. They adorned the rendered façades of many of the sixteenth-century *palazzi*, propping up corner grates, inhabiting triangular pediments over huge, ornate front doors. The sight of these parentless infants cavorting in the shadows of the dimly lit street was disorientating. It was as though the city's foundling past was beckoning, inviting us to enter its dolorous world.

I saw her again: the midwife, whooshing past with her precious cargo strapped to her body. The carriage would have dropped them at the city's western gates. Porta delle Lame, let's say. In an earlier era, it had two drawbridges for wagons and pedestrians and connected the city to the swampy plains. It was late afternoon in December, around four pm, and the air was gelid. There was a grey mist about, and a tinge of barely perceptible violet laced the dark sky. Or perhaps it was sleeting, snowing even, and the bare trees and piazzas were coated in a thick layer of white powder. The icy flecks would have stuck to the folds of Rosa's outer garments as she hastened towards San Procolo, the location of the foundling home, a brisk twenty-five-minute walk from the city periphery, longer through the slushy snow.

Hidden from view, the tiny, swaddled bundle was tucked inside a sling made of hemp cloth and concealed by Rosa's heavy midnight-coloured cloak. Baby Natalina would have been famished, weak and silent, having been deprived of milk. She was born early that morning, half past nine, so Rosa reported to the priest, and her only sustenance was likely the mashed chestnuts her mother had prepared for their journey. I saw Rosa pause to push the last of the mush into the child's mouth with her pinkie finger. Hardly suitable nourishment for a newborn; no surprise many foundlings perished on such journeys.

Rosa knew where she was headed, having made this journey a dozen times that year on similar missions. She may have noticed the transformations taking place at the time: the city was expanding, and workers would soon begin tearing down the medieval walls. On she continued, following the watercourses that still snaked through Bologna. They were the city's lifeblood, as well as the places people went to cleanse their clothes and themselves: a pulsating network of canals linking the urban centre to the countryside, delivering goods, powering mills.

She kept her head down to prevent the small daggers of ice pricking her cheeks; how grateful she would have been to enter the shelter of the porticoes. Her long skirts swished about her worn leather boots, which were wet from misstepping in dirty puddles. She would dry the waterlogged toes by the embers when she returned home to her family in San Giovanni later that night.

The baby, on the other hand, wretched creature, was about to spend her first parentless Christmas in the God-forsaken world of the foundling home.

We had dinner that first night at Da Lucia, a cosy restaurant and wine bar on Via Broccaindosso, a street that has kept its name since the thirteenth century. It is thought the name originated from the tree branches used to beat the donkeys that once carried loads of rocks and earth along the street. Either that or it was named for a family who participated in the Crusades, led by the pope against enemies of the faith.

We sat at an outdoor table, where we shivered in the late autumn air because it seemed easier than taking the wheelchair inside, and ate traditional cuisine: *balanzoni*, a green, mortadella-filled tortellini, and *ragù alla Bolognese*, requesting spaghetti instead of the traditional tagliatelle on the menu. Later, the proprietor informed me, good-naturedly, I had committed 'a real sacrilege' in the city that invented the dish.

All the while I told myself that it was my great-grandmother's city, that I should feel connected to this place. One of the few memories my mother had of Natalina was that she was a wonderful cook, and here I was, sampling the foods she would have grown up cooking (Bologna's other nickname is La Grassa, 'the fat one'). I had arrived in Bologna half believing the city already existed inside me, a latent presence embedded deep in my DNA or wherever memories of ancestors are stored. But I felt no stirrings of recognition during that first meal. It occurred to me that I hadn't grown up hearing stories about Bologna as I had of my mother's birth city, Trieste, which existed strongly in my mind from the time I was a child. Bologna was never mentioned.

After dinner we returned to Via Parigi, retracing our steps along the yellow-lit porticoes. Our apartment was in a modern red-brick building, wedged between a pharmacy and a hairdresser. We took the lift to the second floor, setting off a neighbour's dog – as would occur every time we came or went from the apartment. The small dog's ferocious barking and its owner's shushing continued until we closed the red front door behind us.

The landlady had been there to greet us when we'd arrived earlier that afternoon. The stylish PR woman with diamante-encrusted sneakers was flanked by her amiable husband and Chinese cleaner. Now the space was ours. I rolled the wheelchair along the smooth, reddish timber floorboards and absorbed the features of the combined kitchen, dining and living room. It was tasteful, generous-sized, with no old-apartment cooking odours. Lived-in, but only by itinerants like us who were subject to the watchful eye of Giuseppina and her wingmen.

To my left on the black island bench at a convenient table height, I saw where I would feed and homeschool our boy. On the floor, between the white modular sofa and the TV, was where he would set up his toy cars while episodes of *Teenage Mutant Ninja Turtles*, dubbed in Italian, played in the background. Down the corridor, in the more generous of the two bathrooms, was the washing machine where I would wash all our clothes. And out on the same level terrace, among the potted herbs, was where I would have conversations with the anthropologists and historians who would help fill in the blanks of Ersilia's life.

Within the white walls of this genial, contemporary apartment, I saw how our family could exist in a world of medieval cobblestones. In here, I could be the mother I wanted to be. Out there, Michael would help me negotiate the city's streets when I needed him to, as he always did. I'd hardly dared believe it, but together, the three of us could make this living-in-Italy frolic work.

3
Instincts

The boy whose cheeks are soft peaches leans his back against the dark pink wall. He stands in the gap between two parked cars, his sneakered feet planted on the large rectangular stones that mark out a path for pedestrians. It is an overcast day, and he wears a black puffer jacket that reaches midway down his thighs, and baggy navy tracksuit pants that are too long for his little legs. A red airline satchel, a gift from the Emirates stewards, is slung across his body. His eyes are lifted upwards, his gaze intense, as he takes in the enormous porticoed structure in front of him across the other side of the narrow cobblestoned street. He sucks his bottom lip with his new, permanent front teeth that have just started to poke through the gum.

He has been told that a distant relative, his grandmother's nonna, lived here once when she was a baby and her parents were unable to look after her. Is he marvelling at the age of the crumbling medieval building with the dirty yellow stucco façade? Counting the thirteen tall arches with red-brick columns? Imagining what lies behind the drawn red window coverings?

The photograph was taken on my iPhone the day we first saw Bologna's foundling home, the institution whose mention in Natalina's birth record betrayed her origins. That initial glimpse, seeing it in the flesh, was spine-tingling for me. I can only guess at what our son, who I'd dragged halfway across the world for this, was thinking. Perhaps: *why has my mamma brought me here?*

The Bastardini is located on a quiet section of Via D'Azeglio, a street that begins at Piazza Maggiore, Bologna's central square, and ends at the site of the southern Porta San Mamolo gate. (The actual gate, an imposing thirteenth-century portal, was unthinkably demolished in 1903.) A circular plaque entitled *Oratorio dei Bastardini* explains that the uncompleted edifice dated to 1500 and was designated a hospice:

> *per I 'bastardini', e cioè per I trovatelli ...*
> for the 'little bastards', that is, the foundlings ...

That word again. In Natalina's day, the use of the term *bastardini* sent a clear signal to married parents, who might otherwise be tempted, that this was a place to leave illegitimate babies only. It is said that *bastardini* was not an offensive term because it derived from the Bolognese dialect and was used in a charitable sense. This might seem more convincing in Milan, where abandoned girls in the local dialect were called *stelline*, 'little stars'. 'Foundling', its inclusion on the plaque implied, was a more palatable term to modern ears than 'little bastard'.

The word 'foundling' made my great-grandmother's birth sound almost romantic. *Webster's* defines foundling as: 'A child found after it has been abandoned by its unknown parents.' It is a softer word, the emphasis being on the finding (the verb *trovare* means 'to find'), the blame for abandonment shared, unlike the word 'bastard' which only makes the father disappear. (As does 'abandoned', which obliterates any consideration of the circumstances that led to the mother's act, absolving every other actor – father, priest, official – of responsibility.) To me, 'foundling' has almost magical connotations, as though the child floated down from the sky, and its parents may never have existed at all. Perhaps this is because the word sounds like 'changeling', those creatures swapped by fairies preying on unbaptised children.

The salmon-pink building behind us was once a maternity hospital, created around the time Ersilia was born, so women could give birth and leave their babies without fear of detection. Beside it was the Gothic-style eleventh-century San Procolo church, with the sort of plain orange-brick face – just a simple cross above a rose window – that made me think of the medieval stonemasons who would have toiled there for decades with their buckets and pickaxes. A century later, the Benedictine monks established the first hospice for abandoned children in this spot. It relied on charity to function and was always starved of funds.

This was the street where sessions of the Council of Trent were held during the Counter-Reformation, while the plague raged in Trento. One of the few figures we had encountered in the previous ten minutes was an elderly monk in white robes. It was not a stretch to summon the foundlings who were once dressed in white cloaks and angels' wings and made to march, like the ghosts of Herod's slaughtered babies, through the streets on the Holy Innocents' Day, begging the wealthy for alms.

In reconstructing Ersilia's story and trying to answer the question of why she gave her daughter away, there was another word whose connotations bothered me: 'maternal', as in having feelings 'typical of a caring mother'. What does it mean to possess 'maternal instinct'? Is it the sense of having a birthright to mother? Is maternal instinct something you are either born with or not – as the word 'instinct' suggests – or can it be acquired? Does believing that you do not have the instinct simply mean you lack confidence in your ability to mother? Or does it indicate a certain ambivalence towards motherhood, hopefully superseded if you do happen to have a child?

When my son calls out 'Mamma', when others refer to me as a 'mum', my heart soars, as though I can't quite believe they mean me. It's an identity that has taken time to feel authentically mine. Like wearing a hat when you've long admired them on other, more confident women, but have never felt self-assured enough to wear one yourself. For so long I feared I would look like a fraud, that others would see through me, when all that matters is what my child feels, that I belong to him: this scarred but determined woman, the only mother he knows.

The truth is, I never felt instinctively 'maternal'. Even before the plane crash, I secretly feared the baby thing would never happen to me. Partly, I suspected God didn't want me to have 'everything' and, having spent my career-swapping twenties hopelessly single, finding a partner and having children seemed like everything.

I was asked to be a bridesmaid six times, but only once to be a godmother (even then, it was my niece, and I missed the baptism due to being in a coma). My friends probably never saw me as being maternal either. I am not the adult at social gatherings who swoops in on the hapless newborn then gathers it up in their arms and proceeds to rock it in a display of motherly adroitness. It makes me nervous to see tiny babies passed back and forth between cooing adults, and I find myself wishing their parents would just hurry up and take them back.

When I was twenty-six, I wrote to a friend who had just announced her first pregnancy that 'I don't really know what to say … the experience is so far off for me – it's like another world'. I went on: 'I can't imagine how I'd feel to be watching and feeling such a transformation happen to me, I can't say that I'm feeling any maternal tendencies in the slightest. Perhaps one day I will?'

I share my early lack of 'maternal instinct' with my mother, who once told me she would do anything for her children but thought she would have made a better 'career woman'. We were at an Italian delicatessen in Concord, in Sydney's inner west, where my mother had just pointed out the Roberts Borotalco talc powder her mother used to like, the Simmenthal tinned beef she used to buy. Mum never had the opportunity, though, to have the career she wanted after her father forced her to leave school at fifteen to help pay the family mortgage. I took her arm to get down the hill to where she had parked the car, unsteady on my prosthetic legs, and her forearm reminded me of my nonna's. Soft, olive-skinned, with plain gold bracelets that jangled whenever she moved her wrist. Afterwards we went for coffee at an Italian *pasticceria* where she told me she was closer to her father than her mother. Nonna always told her she was the more robust of her two daughters, and I got the sense Mum wore this as you might wear a medal you never wanted to win – like the religion award I won at the end of Year Twelve – which hangs too heavy around your neck.

For most of my life, my sense of self has been disproportionately reflected in my mother's judgement of me. While I've always cared too much about what others think, hers has forever been the good opinion I've worked hardest for.

My mother came to Australia from Italy with her family when she was nine, and she has never recovered from the dislocation and prejudice she experienced. Almost ten years ago I asked my mother to talk about her formative immigrant experiences. It was eye-opening for me, and I was sure that her having shared them and me having really listened – rather than trying to shield myself from her wounds, as I had done in the past – would grant me what I craved from her: true emotional connection.

This was a turning of the tables; growing up, I was conscious of my mother wanting greater intimacy with me. Yet through my teens and twenties I held back, retreated into myself, not trusting in her responses were I to share the matters of my heart. I knew it hurt her that I would not. When I had my child, something shifted in me.

Sometime after our talk, I told my mother I believed that understanding her immigrant childhood better would help deepen our relationship.

'We don't have a relationship,' my mother responded. 'I'm your mother; you're my daughter.'

At the time it felt like the worst rejection, annihilating even: my own mother saying she doesn't have – or doesn't want? – a relationship with me. Did she mean ours was a random pairing, two people thrown together, not of their own choosing? Or did she see no separation between us?

One Saturday morning I waited out the front of our house for my parents to pick me up in their car. I was taking them to my favourite plant nursery, around the corner from where we lived. When I first discovered the nursery, shortly after we moved in at the start of 2018, I immediately knew that I wanted to take my mother there, anticipating that she would love it. But, being located in the back garden of the owner's house, not to mention the subsequent COVID lockdowns, its opening hours had been erratic. Finally, we found a date when the nursery would be open and we were all free. I felt uplifted by a childish excitement that I was doing something good for my mother, that she was about to experience joy.

My father parked the car outside the front of the nursery, and we clambered out. Wambling unsteadily down the hidden stony laneway lined with epiphytic plants, I watched my mother's eyes light up. After we entered the cool, shaded garden at the other end, with its shelves of whimsical bird statues, pots of succulents, misty terrariums and dripping water features, I asked her what she thought. I brimmed with expectation.

She mentioned the name of a close friend of hers from church. 'She will love this. I must bring her here.' She glanced around, looked behind her. 'When is it open next? I'm going to ask the owner.'

It was the tiniest of slights, but still I was deflated. My moment had been hijacked. Not a word, then or after, acknowledging the meaning in that act of my sharing a place *I* loved with her. Why couldn't she see me? And why did I so desperately need to be seen? The rational part of me said my mother's conception of parenthood was authoritarian, and I was her subordinate. This reflected her own upbringing. Still, I felt flattened.

Shortly after, I read American novelist Richard Ford's memoir about his parents and was startled to read him ask: 'Does one ever have a "relationship" with one's mother? I think not.' This was followed by: 'Love, which is never typical, sheltered everything. We expected it to be reliable, and it was.'

It occurred to me that the word 'relationship' might mean something different to my mother than it did to me. Perhaps, like Ford, she too understood her role as a mother to be utterly reliable and constant and maybe, for her, this transcended any relationship. It was possible that in her eyes, maternal love was bigger than anything the word 'relationship' – which implied two souls coming together, not two souls already entwined – could embody. Whereas Ersilia cast off her daughter, my mother had subsumed me into herself. How could you 'see' the other person when she was so wholly conjoined with yourself?

A friend with grown daughters once told me that when children become teenagers, they must learn to despise their mothers, so that they can separate themselves. When I obtained a full-time job in a legal firm, after finishing the College of Law, I moved out of home for the first time and for six months shared a house on a steep hill near the Lane Cove National Park with three friends and two rambunctious Labradors. My mother refused to visit that house. Her anger was like white heat. I felt cast out. Because I had dared to leave home, she pulled down the shutters on me. I assumed it was because she was used to having control over me, that she understood my radical assertion of independence as an act of disobedience. I was twenty-three.

Recently she told me how hurt she had been by the suddenness of my departure, which came about without consultation or discussion. (I only remember my eagerness to be gone.) After she had put me through six years of law school, sheltered me, shopped for me, cooked my meals, washed my dishes, sheets, towels and clothes, thrown me a surprise welcome-home-from-backpacking-in-South-America party with all my friends, and everything else, the first thing I did once installed in my shiny new career was to pack up and leave without warning. For my mother, having found me bound to her unmaternal self, my wanting to separate from her in this way must have felt like the worst ingratitude.

There is a line in Anne Enright's novel *The Wren, The Wren*, about a mother and daughter, that resonated with me: 'She gave me her whole life, she told me once, *her whole life*, and I said, Fuck you, fuck you, fuck you, fuck you, fuck you.' I like the ambiguity, the meaning that alters depending on whose perspective you read it from, the mother's or the daughter's. 'Fuck you, I don't care that you gave me your whole life.' Or: 'Fuck you, for trying to make me feel bad.'

I realised it was possible that, given the urgency with which as a teenager and young woman I sought liberation from my family – that determination to be 'free and whole' – my mother simply feels that I ask too much of her now.

Maybe the unreasonable one is me.

To the right of the Bastardini building was a staircase that connected the foundling home, with its elevated portico, to the street. It had to be the same one Rosa Rizzi climbed that cold December afternoon, the day Ersilia gave her daughter away. What relief Rosa must have felt when she reached it. Having been on her feet since the early hours, she could finally discharge her fragile burden.

What I knew of Rosa was contained in a dossier the San Giovanni in Persiceto volunteers had given me. She was fifty-three when she delivered Natalina and would only live six more years. She was the town's most important midwife and could read and write. She had lived in San Giovanni her whole life and married a local man, a waiter. Together they had fourteen children, seven of each sex, half of whom did not survive early childhood. More than twenty years of her life were spent pregnant – if the children were all biological. Midwives sometimes kept foundlings, so they may not have all been.

From these bare facts, I compiled a portrait. Rosa had her own fair share of tragedy and likely never grieved more than when she lost her eighth child, aged six. I hypothesised this because Luigia's was the only name she reused, giving it to the next girl to be born. Her life coaxing babies into the world was filled with purpose – but would have worn her down. There was the broken sleep, the knocks on the door in the middle of the night and the familiar figure on the stoop, uttering: 'It is time.' And the difficult cases, the women for whom conception was traumatic, and motherhood impossible. Women who wept when they heard their baby's first cry, who she had to console while wrapping the tiny, waxy bodies, assuring the mothers who would never hold them, 'It is better this way.'

Overshadowing this, Rosa may have felt conflicted because, as a midwife, she was not only an ally of women, but also a set of eyes for the provincial authorities. Long viewed with suspicion by the Church, midwives were ingeniously brought under its control during the Counter-Reformation by giving them emergency baptism powers to administer the sacrament to babies in danger of dying. Rosa was required to report all illegitimate pregnancies to foundling home officials, who recorded them in the *Libro delle Denunce*, the 'Book of Denunciation'. If she failed to do this or – God forbid – helped a woman do away with an unwanted one, she could have lost her licence to practise, be fined and even jailed. Rosa had no choice in this, her two faces.

In Bologna, midwives formed a central part of a network of informants the Church established in the 1500s and tightened over subsequent centuries to spy on pregnant women. The objective was to ensure the babies of unmarried mothers – whether girlfriends, lovers, domestic servants, factory workers, rape victims, sufferers of incest, or prostitutes – were brought to term. The Church co-opted priests, midwives and police, as well as landlords, neighbours, employers and officials into its scheme. I imagined these watchers, peeking through windows, lurking in corridors, hanging about the market stalls and water fountains, their eyes all trained on women's bellies, watching for the tell-tale signs of scandal. If women were considered at risk of not proceeding with their pregnancies, police transferred them to the House of Correction where they were jailed until the birth, after which their illegitimate offspring were deposited in foundling homes.

I left the wheelchair at the bottom of the stairs on the corner of Via D'Azeglio and Via San Procolo. Entering beneath the first arch, I gripped the cold metal railing with my right hand and pulled myself up the ten stone steps, channelling Rosa's fatigue, the weary clump of her boots. On the final step I stretched out my hand to touch the yellow-rendered brick wall and thought of her steadying herself at the end of her 30-kilometre journey, feeling the baby's heart faintly beating against her own. I imagined Rosa checking her pockets for the rag in which Ersilia had wrapped the *elemosina*, the foundling home's dues for leaving one's baby. In a moment the midwife would hand over the money and then, finally, the starving child could be delivered to one of the pitiable live-in wet nurses to be fed. The little girl would be out of both their lives forever.

There were never enough of these women – live-in wet nurses – for the number of foundlings. Their milk was critical to the babies' survival since there were no safe means of bottle-feeding. But who would want the job? The Bastardini came up with a solution to the problem of recruitment. Women abandoning their babies were required to pay a fee, or else be forced to serve a year inside the foundling home as a wet nurse.

Conditions were arduous. The wet nurses lived in the same room as the babies. They nursed multiple foundlings at a time – though never their own. They were not permitted to leave the foundling home to visit friends or family. If it sounds like these impecunious women were being punished for sexual transgressions, many in the day viewed it that way too. (After Italian Unification, some of the restrictions on them were relaxed slightly.) These live-in wet nurses were the poorest of the poor, society's most disadvantaged, isolated and marginalised women, sometimes – though not always – prostitutes. They were often sickly and passed on their illnesses to the malnourished babies.

We walked the length of the portico, across the speckled stone tiles that were the colour of a riverbed, searching for an open door. This was where Natalina had spent the first three months of her life. I wanted to find the room where her crib had stood, to linger in the space where she'd slept, fed and cried. To conjure the chaos that had surrounded her, the wails of all those cold and hungry infants laid out in rows like swaddled, tinned fish. The stone floors, the brick walls, the high, sloped ceilings: they too remembered. I thought that if I could explore inside, I might pick up on some of the immanent energy – the heavy sadness – that had dispersed, seeped, bled into the material structures that once enveloped those motherless babies. Doing so could bring me closer to understanding Natalina's experience.

What other remnants existed? There were no photographs from inside the Bastardini taken in the days when it operated. The only plans I found showed the layout of the rooms as they appeared in 1667. They placed the wet nurses' quarters at the back of the complex of buildings, behind a room marked 'oven' (maybe it was warmer there). From books, I knew conditions inside were unhealthy: intense cold, noxious air, filthy linen, rampant disease, inadequate milk, the excrement of wandering goats underfoot.

We couldn't find a way in. The tall, heavy, dark timber doors were locked, barring our entry like a drawbridge raised against an enemy. The building appeared abandoned; in fact, the provincial government was auctioning it off to developers to be turned into upmarket residences and commercial office space. Retracing our steps along the portico, I noticed a terracotta mould behind a grate that also covered a window. Two swaddled babies were crossed over each other, forming an 'X'. The babies were tightly bound, like tiny mummies. These foundling babies were revered, but disposable. ('X' on historical documents indicates a person is deceased.) Here was my remnant.

Seeing that terracotta mould, I thought of the Silvia Plath poem 'Tulips', about the red flowers in a hospital room that could be heard breathing through their gift paper, 'Lightly, through their white swaddlings, like an awful baby.' That ambiguous pairing of words – 'awful' as in dreaded? or 'awful' as in awe-inspiring? – that hinted at a mother with unspeakably unmaternal thoughts. Thoughts which may not have been unmaternal at all.

I was always too frightened to swaddle our son; my husband did it. We had enough muslin wraps of ethereal pastel organic cotton for every day of the week, and it was my task to wash and fold and stack them on the shelf beneath the timber change table. It was a division of labour that felt safe to me. I did not trust myself, swaddling from a wheelchair (God forbid I do it incorrectly and accidentally strangle him). Michael, who had never handled a muslin sheath before in his life, folded and wrapped and tucked and smoothed the fabric around our newborn with the kind of confidence and dexterity I could never muster. Why was I so scared of doing harm?

I have big gaps in my memory of my son's toddler years. I took six months' maternity leave from my doctoral studies after he was born, but getting back to the thesis was never far from my mind. Michael, who gave up full-time work to look after our baby, remembers my non-negotiable daily 'minimums', sometimes hours, sometimes word limits. To guarantee my required periods of solitude, I found things for them to do outside the house, activities that would have been difficult, if not impossible, for me to do independently with a small child. 'Baby Play' at a local pool. Questacon (the science museum). 'Giggle and Wiggle' at the Woden Library. 'Music for Everyone'. The Steiner school playgroup with the broken tea pots and knitted hats. The miniature railway.

In 2017, shortly before we moved from Canberra to Sydney, the three of us attended a birthday party in Weston Park, the home of *Bluebell*, the miniature train that L had loved as a toddler. It was a beautiful spring day, with families gathering under the large trees and rowers and ducks on the nearby lake.

'Why have we not come here more often?' I asked Michael.

He replied that he and L had visited the park many times in the days before our son started school. He had lots of memories of L as a two-year-old, of the two of them sitting at the kiosk by the *Bluebell* ticket office, eating ice-creams. They had done this nearly every week.

These are memories I do not have.

I've sometimes wondered why I spent those precious years madly finishing the doctorate, completing a post-doc, beginning another one. The truth is the intensive academic work demanding my time and attention was a distraction, a way to lessen the pain I felt because I could not take my toddler to all those activities on my own.

Oh, the number of times I have wished I still had my pre-crash body. That I could grab L's hand, an armful of buckets and spades and towels, and take him down to the sand on some beach to explore the rockpools together. Instead of having to ask someone else – Michael, my mother, my sister – to take him for me.

It's not to deny that I derived purpose and enjoyment from the university work; I did. But it was also a form of self-protection.

Today some of our son's sporting activities are in such inhospitable places for a mother with limited mobility that it is often easier to let Michael handle this part of our parenting. Sometimes parking is far away; there are multiple fields, and we'd have to traverse vast distances in long grass to reach the right one; there is a hill to climb. Or the swimming pool's surrounds are slippery; the indoor cricket nets are upstairs and there is no lift; or the day is too warm, and I would suffer inside my prosthetics. I fill those weekend mornings with writing or tending to my indoor plants. These activities distract me from the frustration that I cannot perform such a simple task as taking my child, on my own, to weekend sport. From the hopelessness I feel that could almost, I sometimes think, descend into despair.

American poet Adrienne Rich wrote about the 'invisible thread' that, as the mother of an infant, would pull taut between them when she tried to do anything for herself. As though the child sensed her gliding into a world that didn't include him and feared abandonment. It made her angry and she craved time alone, even a few minutes, telling herself if she got it, she would be able to 'love so much better'. According to Rich, this 'emotion-charged, tradition-heavy' form of motherhood she found herself in was not a 'natural phenomenon'.

Perhaps in reaction to the way I was mothered, I resist the idea that my child is an extension of me. But this introduces a fresh anxiety: too much distance. Having left academia, I am more present in some ways because I am rarely absent from home. I am there for every bedtime and wake-up, send-off and welcome home from school, every breakfast, afternoon tea and dinner. In other ways, however – away from the house, in social situations, when our family is exposed to the gaze of others – I am less present.

I think of Ersilia, of the constraints that made her believe she was unable to mother her child: religion, shame, poverty. Was my hands-off mothering during L's toddler and pre-school years a kind of abandonment too, not through choice, but physical constraints? I am haunted by a fear that the distance my disability creates between my son and me will someday be misunderstood, that it will be mistaken for indifference. Like I didn't try hard enough.

Would the child survive the week? Rosa may have wondered, handing Natalina over to the Bastardini officials. Her odds were not good. Foundling homes in nineteenth-century Italy were regarded as institutions for killing children at the public's expense. My great-grandmother had a one-in-four chance of living to her first birthday. I know this because, serendipitously, she was born during a significant moment for the Bastardini hospital, and historians have expounded at length about the episode.

The work of American scholar David Kertzer and others helped solve a mystery in Natalina's foundling home file. It explained why it took officials three months to place her with a paid wet nurse in the community. This, when getting babies out of the unsanitary foundling home, where they risked dying of starvation or disease, was considered urgent to their survival.

Natalina was assigned to the wet nurse Maria Benassi and her husband, Augusto Sabattino, in late March 1899. They were farmhands from the foothills of the Apennines in a place called Gorgognano. Their personal details and all their payments were set out in a large book called the *Campionario delle Balie*, the wet-nurse register, now preserved at Bologna's Archivio Storico Provinciale.

Maria was not what the foundling home would have considered an ideal community wet nurse, but she came close. The Bastardini sought women with good quality milk who were not feeding their own child and hence would not neglect the foundling (meaning Maria's own baby had probably recently died). They had to be from the country – not the city, which was considered corrupt – and preferably from the closer-in hills, not the mountains with their harsh climate. Tick, tick. The Bastardini, however, also preferred sharecroppers to farmhands, because they were wealthier and had the support of extended family to care for the foundling while the woman worked. Maria fell short on this measure. But the foundling home could not afford to be so picky, particularly during this trying period when attracting country wet nurses was especially difficult for one reason: syphilis.

By the 1890s, the sexually transmitted disease had become a grave issue for Bologna's foundling home. Syphilitic babies, many of them children of prostitutes, were passing the disease onto country wet nurses through mouth sores, and the women were giving it to their own families.

In 1892 one of these women, whose own children had died from syphilis after she contracted the disease from a sickly foundling, successfully sued the Bastardini hospital. Fearing more expensive payouts, the foundling home issued a new policy. Because it was impossible to diagnose hereditary syphilis in newborns, with symptoms taking three months to appear, it was decided to keep all foundlings under observation during this period. Foundlings unable to be fed by their own mothers (by now the Bastardini had done away with the rule preventing this) had to be fed by artificial means, usually cow's or goat's milk, meaning multitudes perished.

Of the 474 babies left at the Bastardini in 1898, almost 60 per cent died. For newborns left without their own mother to feed them, as Natalina was, the mortality rate was close to 75 per cent.

Natalina's foundling home file contained her mother's health questionnaire, devised to establish whether she had syphilis. Questions like: did she have white marks in her mouth or throat, had she lost a lot of hair recently, experienced fevers, used mercury treatments, noticed white scars in the baby's placenta? Ersilia answered no to all; she was healthy; she was also, we can infer from this, not a prostitute.

Nevertheless, Natalina had to wait out those three perilous months. I imagined her waking up next to undiscovered cadavers; mass burials of dead babies taking place outside the foundling home every week.

A Bologna historian would later tell me the issue of syphilis for foundlings and their wet nurses was a 'devastating phenomenon', undervalued by historians, 'much worse than the plague'. Ultimately the powerful Bologna nobility, who had run the Bastardini with great self-interest for centuries – many of the illegitimate babies were their own, born to their domestic servants – 'managed' the problem.

'These are things about which there is no memory,' he told me.

After I began investigating Natalina's story, my mother gave me an antique metal pin box. It was round and tarnished, with a dented base. She had used it to store sewing pins, needles threaded with bitten-off pieces of cotton, spare school-uniform and business-shirt buttons. (She made clothes for my sister and me when we were young: pretty dresses of pink and yellow, from puckered seersucker cotton).

I recalled the pin box from when I was a child, how I had liked to prise it open to see what hidden treasures – pins with pearly heads, brass thimbles – it contained. I never knew it had once belonged to my great-grandmother.

On the lid of the box was an intricate engraving of a scene of winged infants. They had round, burnished bellies, were holding hands and dancing. I counted eight of them beneath the wide canopy of a tree in whose branches another five or so babies lolled about. It looked as though the infants were partaking in some secret ceremony. As a child, I thought it was a kind of corroboree or faerie dance. But now, I wondered if perhaps they were *putti*.

I held the box in my palm, pressing the cold babies into my flesh, making them warm. I speculated how the pin box came into Natalina's possession, whether she had chosen it for the decoration on the lid, a representation of what she nearly was: an angel baby.

Missing from the front entrance during our stroll that day was the Bastardini's foundling wheel. It was thought to have once been positioned at the opposite end of the portico to the staircase. If so, it would have sat underneath a fresco of the Madonna with her child and adjacent to a frightening wrought-iron gargoyle with female features and a canine head, known as La Diavolessa. Together, these discordant images would have simultaneously comforted and censured any mothers attempting to use the wheel.

Unlike many other Italian cities (including Florence), Bologna had a low tolerance for the foundling wheel. This was mainly because mothers using it could avoid paying the fee, but also because it was thought to facilitate the abandonment of legitimate children. The wheel led directly into the guardian's room and allowed women to leave children at the hospital without being seen. The role of guardian was usually held by a husband and wife, who slept in the *stanza della ruota*, the 'room of the wheel'.

What became of Bologna's wheel nobody knows, although a foundling wheel of uncertain provenance was discovered in 2017 in the deposits of the Baraccano, formerly the site of a sixteenth-century conservatory for orphaned girls. It was put on display at La Quadreria, a local art gallery. Some believe it is the same specimen that once featured at the front of the Bastardini hospital and was in use until the late nineteenth century.

Reading about foundling wheels, I was intrigued to come across the 1877 painting *The Guard at the Foundling Wheel*, by Neapolitan artist Gioacchino Toma, which hangs in the National Gallery of Modern and Contemporary Art in Rome. Two women guards sit on wooden chairs either side of a wall cavity that houses a foundling wheel; the rotating chamber is lined with bedding, like a cradle. The hour is late – an oil lamp casts heavy shadows across the walls, furniture and floor of the cavernous receiving room – and the guards have fallen asleep. A swaddled baby, its pink hands free and raised into the air, lies on a large bed, shoved into the corner so it can't roll off. It looks forlorn, like a discarded package.

The painting's most startling feature, what makes it so curious, is the pair of small holes cut into the cavity, which shine like the eyes of an animal in the dark. The holes are there for the guards to peer through, to catch mothers trying to leave their babies without paying the necessary alms. But those smouldering orbs seem to stare out of the painting as though it is the guards who are being watched – and not only them.

Having initially been so appalled at the idea of the foundling wheel, I was surprised to discover they are still used all over the world, including in Italy, the US, Germany, Canada and elsewhere, though not Australia. Today's baby hatches (or havens) tend to be temperature-controlled cradles monitored with sensors and alarms to alert medical staff. They are located at hospitals, sometimes churches and police and fire stations. With cameras positioned only at the baby's bed, these cradles permit anonymous abandonment.

The harsh reality is babies are still left 'exposed' – on doorsteps, outside medical centres, on beaches, in parks, inside drains. Proponents of baby hatches argue they offer a more humane option, not only protecting the babies but also giving agency to the vulnerable mothers compelled to use them. Their use, however, remains controversial, with claims they are 'medieval' and breach children's international human rights to know their parents.

Every so often there are calls in Australia for the introduction of baby hatches. This happened in 2016 after the body of a baby girl was discovered buried on Maroubra Beach in Sydney. I was moved by the Deputy Coroner's description of the unknown mother. Poverty, the stigma of teen pregnancies, and some cultures' preference for male children were common factors in child abandonment, he said. The mother's actions suggested she was 'ashamed, vulnerable, and scared' and needed 'help and understanding rather than cheap and shallow criticism'. He continued, 'If the lesson we teach these women is that they are lepers in our midst, what incentive is there for them to seek help for their babies and themselves?'

Immediately I thought of those eyes in Toma's painting. Separated by centuries, the artist and the coroner both inverted the spotlight from the mother, whom society sought to shame, onto society itself.

We visited La Quadreria one day to see Bologna's wheel. It sat on a perspex stand in the middle of a room with arched ceilings, billowing white curtains and a speckled pink stone floor. It looked like a wine barrel with a large hole cut in one side, which was big enough for my son to climb into.

The Bastardini building is ragged with its imperfect, Tuscan-inspired portico. The exposed and weathered bricks above the arches have the look of cardboard that rodents have chewed through.

In truth, the portico is unfinished. It was the vision of Giovanni II Bentivoglio, the tyrannical nobleman who ruled Bologna for sixty-five years. He began redeveloping the foundling home in 1480; the portico was the centrepiece. A power struggle with the Catholic Church saw his family expelled in 1506, when Bologna became a Papal State. As a result, the works on the foundling home were never completed.

Bologna's foundling home continued operating all the way through the first half of the twentieth century. It finally became redundant in the decades after World War II, following a series of legal changes in Italy during the 1970s that transformed women's lives. They included giving women access to the contraceptive pill, legal abortion and kindergartens, as well as decriminalising adultery and introducing no-fault divorce. By 1990, no children were entering the foundling home, and it shut its doors.

Viewing the Bastardini building in person that day, finding it bolted shut and uninhabited, a hollow husk with no obvious effort to preserve its history, left me feeling kind of empty too. It seemed incredible that the city could sell off its foundling hospital when Florence, by contrast, had transformed its own institution into a celebrated museum, Museo degli Innocenti.

The Innocenti, as Florence's foundling home was known, was designed by Renaissance architect Filippo Brunelleschi (who also created the city's *duomo*). While the Bastardini is orange and red and crumbly, the Innocenti is the colour of bones and fully rendered. The museum was restored in 2016 and in the halls where wet nurses once roamed, you now encounter works by Renaissance painters Botticelli and Ghirlandaio, along with detailed accounts of the city's treatment of its abandoned children.

When we set our departure date for Italy, back in Sydney, L informed me he didn't want to go. He would rather stay behind with his grandparents.

'We have to trust that Mummy knows what she's doing,' Michael had told him.

Seeing the Bastardini hospital, I thought that if I had to explain to my son why I took him all the way to Bologna to see such a seemingly unremarkable place, I would say something like this:

'This building has stood here for eight hundred years. It forms part of the history of the Catholic religion I have imposed on you, and of how it treated (and still treats) women. It is an important part of the history of the women in your family. That history is incomplete, with gaps I will never be able to fill, but it is one worth remembering. It is my history, and it is yours. Since there is no Bastardini museum to carefully set out any of this history for us, this scruffy building can only mutter it, like an old beggar weighed down by stories nobody wants to know. If we listen hard enough, we will hear what the old man is trying to say.'

4
Inheritance

There are patterns in our maternal line – weak hearts, a sense of being untethered – that could be traced, if you believe that sort of thing, back to Ersilia. In a cumbrous black book that an Italian cousin recommended to me, *Metagenealogy* (subtitle: *Self-Discovery through Psychomagic and the Family Tree*), I read that heart problems in genealogy suggest a lack of love, a feeling of doubting one's right to be.

Natalina, who grew up without a mother's love, was killed by a heart attack at fifty-eight. Her daughter, my nonna Anna, suffered angina: chest pain caused by reduced blood flow to the heart. The sensation is variously described as squeezing, pressure, heaviness, tightness. I imagine a hand, wrapped around her heart. Both of Anna's sisters as well as her two daughters have also inherited heart issues.

The ungroundedness is similarly acute: it is cascading, existential. It begins with Natalina, cast out from San Giovanni in Persiceto at birth, being denied roots. This untying to place was demonstrated when she boldly left Bologna in her early twenties and moved to Trieste. All Natalina's daughters carried their mother's restlessness within them. The three young women, encouraged by the wider post-World War II exodus from Trieste, migrated to Australia after her death, leaving behind their widowed father, who remarried.

Forsaking Italy in the 1950s was entirely my grandmother's decision. Unlike Anna, her husband was deeply attached to their extended family, home, city, country. Their daughters were too. Perhaps they intuited something Anna did not: how unsettling the loss of kin, language and culture would be. Or maybe they didn't carry the same burdens she did. Those burdens of inheritance.

For Alfredo and his daughters, especially my mother as the eldest, the leaving was traumatic. The arriving too. In Australia, my grandparents' marriage came under great strain. Things became so bad, my nonno tried to take his family back to Italy. But that proved impossible, so they stayed.

I wonder what Anna was hoping to find by leaving Italy. She felt suffocated in Trieste, living with her husband's parents. Was she seeking separation from her in-laws or was she running away from something bigger, more existential?

As new migrants, the family of four moved into a terrace in Paddington in Sydney's inner east owned by another Italian. They shared it with four other families and had just the one bedroom to themselves. I try to imagine the intensity of living in that house: so many families living in such small confines, the trouble that must have brewed. A cauldron of instability and strong emotions.

Alfredo found a physically arduous job cutting cane in Queensland. It meant lengthy separations from Anna and their daughters, who got on with things. The girls attended the local Catholic school during the day, and at night the three of them took English classes with members of the other families.

It was while living in that single room in Paddington that my mother stumbled upon her parents' marriage certificate and discovered the real reason they wed. Not love, but an illegitimate pregnancy had forced Anna into marrying.

Until my mother found the marriage certificate, she had believed her parents' story that the couple met soon after the war ended and wed a full year before she was born, but it turned out it was only three months. Her mother conceived her on a drunken New Year's Eve. When her father learnt his unmarried daughter was with child, he threw her out of the house.

I don't know where Anna's mind wandered to at this juncture: what alternative scenarios she may have contemplated; what wild thoughts she might have entertained. I only know that, faced with exile from her family, she married my grandfather.

It took me a while to see the pattern. How, unlike Ersilia, she would not repeat it. It's not like Anna had many choices – but she did have a man who wanted to marry her. Anna would not abandon her daughter.

I already knew the tale of the discovered marriage certificate. Learning about Natalina's origins, however, cast it in a new light, gave it a new significance. Although I was previously aware of my nonna's reticence to wed Alfredo, I had never paused to reflect on how powerless she must have felt upon finding herself unmarried and pregnant to a man she didn't love.

I rethought the few anecdotes I had collected about Anna over the years. Previously I had dismissed them as idiosyncratic, but inconsequential. Now I understood them as clues pointing to a hidden interior life.

There was the blonde doll she brought with her from Italy, a gift from a girlfriend who married an American serviceman. She brushed its hair with great tenderness, starched its dresses, wouldn't let her daughters touch it. I cannot picture the doll, but I do remember my grandparents' separate bedrooms. I reach back, but the memories are fuzzy. I see something propped up on Anna's bed but cannot make it out. The doll?

There was also the romance fiction she devoured. Thousands of Mills & Boon–type paperbacks. I remember there was always a small pile of them on the sideboard in the kitchen, another beside the gaudy black-and-gold sofa in the living room. When she died, we didn't find a journal where she'd written down her thoughts. Instead, there was a black, faux leather diary where she'd assiduously recorded every one of these romances by title, in Italian.

Pondering what these peculiarities might mean, I am reminded of Tennessee Williams' reclusive character Laura Wingfield, with her hopeless crush on high school hero Jim O'Connor. And her beloved glass menagerie, through which she created a gentler, more welcoming yet illusory world.

How far did Anna's imaginary world extend? Here I find myself in that liminal territory again – writing 'at the limit of the unspeakable and the unknown'. Do I dare to ponder on the page? Is it unfair of me to speculate, now she is gone?

It was in Paddington that the marriage teetered, nearly collapsed. Ultimately, however, it survived. My grandparents found a larger rental – one they didn't have to share with other families. Eventually they bought their own house, watched their daughters grow up, had grandchildren. But the imprint of those difficult, unspeakable years has been felt across the generations ever since.

I cherished my nonna. She was a gentle, loving, generous woman whom I saw every weekend for my entire childhood. After our Saturday spaghetti Bolognese lunches, we all played a version of gin rummy at her kitchen table, adults and children.

To console me after I'd lost another game, she used to tell me: 'Unlucky at cards, lucky in love.' As a teenager, I didn't know what to make of the proverb or prediction or whatever it was. It never really heartened me. I would have preferred to win the occasional card game.

After my nonno died, in 1993 (Anna outlived him by sixteen years), I wrote about my grief in a letter to a friend.

> I have this beautiful photo of Nonna on my desk, taken when she must have been 20 years old. It's one of those brown, old photos. The dedication on it is to my grandfather, it says *'Al mio Al, con tutto il mio amore, Anna'*. i.e., to my Al, with all my love, Anna.

I was twenty years old myself when I wrote that letter. And I have no doubt that, in the end, my grandparents did love each other. But I realise how mistaken I had been in assuming the affection between them was uncomplicated.

How much of our mothering is inherited, predetermined by the mothers who came before us and the way they mothered? I'm not talking only about the previous generation, but earlier ones too.

Recently I came across a case study in epigenetics analysing mothering behaviour in rats. It got me ruminating over my own early mothering behaviour. Epigenetics is the process whereby environmental factors affect how genes work, turning them on or off. Perhaps unsurprisingly, scientists have found that mother rats (called dams) who lick and groom their newborn pups a great deal create less anxious offspring than ones who don't. Where epigenetics comes into it is that the licking and grooming triggers a mechanism in the pup's brain, causing the genes responsible for producing receptors for stress hormones to make more of them. These receptors bind the stress hormones, dampening anxiety levels and creating less fearful pups. How attentively a rat mother behaves towards her baby depends on how she has experienced the world in her lifetime, with a scared dam hardly licking and grooming her babies at all. The baby becomes tuned to the danger level of the mother's environment by her behaviour and by epigenetics, effectively inheriting her perception of the world.

I couldn't sleep that night after reading about the mother rats. I wondered if the plane crash had stopped me from properly mothering our son. The traumatic experience had undoubtedly given me an altered view of the world as a dangerous place. Had I unconsciously passed this onto our child, burdened him with it?

I tossed and turned, woke up Michael to ask him, 'What was the lasting impact on L that, in the first days of his life, I was so afraid to mother him?' I remembered how during my pregnancy I was so scared of something going wrong, I refused to believe I was having a baby until he was laid across my chest in the delivery room.

Here was an unbearable thought: that the fear that prevented me from believing in the existence of my foetus could affect my child's perspective on his place in the world. It seems a crazy kind of medieval thinking; to imagine that through my own thoughts I had carved out the character of my unborn child. A saner person would probably advise me to stop punishing myself, but I could not help wondering, was my fear of the world his inheritance?

The mothering behaviour of rats gets passed on to the second or even third generation, with female pups licking and grooming their own offspring according to how their mothers mothered them. Inevitably this sets up a chain. I thought of Ersilia, and realised here was another thing we probably shared. Something, I intuited, had happened in her pre-child-bearing years that made her see the world as such a dangerous place she could not mother her daughter. I knew why *I* thought the world was perilous, but why did she?

We are not born as blank pages upon which anything can be written, Triestine author Susanna Tamaro writes, but rather as tablecloths into which somebody has already woven a pattern. It makes sense that the way Natalina was (un)mothered would affect the way the women who came after her mothered.

When my mother shares that she regrets not telling her mother more often that she loved her, I recognise that her behaviours were likely influenced by the way she was mothered, by how she saw her mother. I understand that when my mother tells me that we don't have a relationship, this is affected by legacies around motherhood inherited from the women who came before.

'Italians never say I love you,' my mother says by way of explanation, and I accept her word. The truth is I feel it too: a yearning to tell my mother I love her, accompanied by an invisible gag preventing me from doing so. But knowing what I do now about Natalina, I also understand that the lives of the women in my family were, unavoidably, created in the pain of Ersilia's abandonment of her daughter. The anguish of Natalina's birth, and whatever circumstances preceded it, her conception, form part of our hidden inheritance. We unknowingly assumed these legacies.

Genetic inheritance, Tamaro also suggests, is like a bomb. Part of our parents, their parents, their parents' parents and so on,

> . . . is closed up inside us as though in a time bomb. But we don't set the timer; it's been set from the beginning, and we know nothing about it. The only wisdom is to be aware that there's something uncontrolled inside us and that at any moment it could explode.

I feared our inheritance from Ersilia, wondered if what happened to her planted bombs inside all of us who came after.

There were those early warnings, my sense of foreboding in relation to how her two illegitimate children came to be. I'd tried to ignore these misgivings, but they were finally brought out into the open one day in Bologna, the worst day, when a local anthropologist connected the dots and gave voice to my darkest fears. In my haste to lay blame for Natalina's abandonment at her mother's feet, I had paid little attention to the father – the man who impregnated her and left her to face the consequences alone – to whom I was also related.

That was about to change.

Nowhere did you feel Bologna's close-quarters living more than on our apartment terrace, where you could hear conversations from the other buildings that all faced inwards onto a common enclosed area. The buildings cast shadows over each other and created a kind of communal inside-outside space, a pocket of shared air invisible from the streets beyond. Noises echoed off the orange external walls. The whirr of a fan, a man talking on his mobile phone, a family chatting in their kitchen with the doors open. Hammering, flapping pigeons, a cat meowing. Somewhere in the distance the wail of a siren, the Italian version a more melodic sound than the shrieks of ambulances back home, like a child's toy.

When the neighbours retreated and the other noises fell silent, a stillness would descend like a blanket. Some of the terraces were enclosed to make greenhouses or drying rooms for hanging washing. Ours was shielded by privacy screens and had a large rectangular glass-topped table with metal legs, which was surrounded by dozens of pots of hardy plants. Roses, oleanders, ferns, cactuses, lavender, rosemary, thyme, strawberries, strappy yuccas, aloe vera. Vines scrambled up trellises. Tropical mandevillas and flowering basil protruded from planter boxes on the balcony railing. I pictured the green oasis that would form in summer. Now though, in autumn, with the low-lying clouds, limp bedsheets, sloping red-tiled roofs and bedraggled plants, the terrace felt confined, the air oppressive.

This day, three of us sat at the table on the terrace: the anthropologist (who asked me not to use her name), my young researcher, Milena, who had arrived in Bologna earlier that morning and would help translate, and me. Michael was at his Italian lesson at Dante Alighieri across the other side of Piazza Maggiore, and L was inside having his own daily language class at the kitchen bench with Valentina, the teacher he and I shared. The anthropologist was friendly, enthusiastic, loquacious, spoke no English but professed an interest in all things Australian. She had worked as a public official and was an expert on the history of Bologna's foundlings.

Our conversation got off to a promising start with an illuminating discussion about the *madrazza*. The word is slang for 'bad mother' and refers to a fictitious, historical illness whereby a woman's menstrual blood, supposedly due to a malfunctioning uterus, was unable to flow around her body and remained inside it, swelling her belly so she looked pregnant – which she was. The *madrazza* functioned as a defence used by women in nineteenth-century Italy accused of infanticide. In practice this was death by abandonment, rather than any violent act. At their legal trials, initiated after their dead babies were discovered, these women claimed to have been unaware they were pregnant, believing they had the *madrazza*.

One of the puzzles of this nonsense disease was that doctors supported the mothers' claims. Who were they protecting? I wondered naïvely. The anthropologist explained that first, this was the state of medical science at the time. Doctors believed in the *madrazza* and prescribed various medicines to cure it. As to whom the doctors were protecting, it was likely the men who had raped these women, because in these proceedings pretty much all the mothers – mostly poor farm girls employed as servants – were victims of rape. A *madrazza* diagnosis absolved the rapists of any accusation of wrongdoing, while preserving the woman's honour and shielding those around her from the disgrace of an illegitimate pregnancy.

'There were always two faces in these stories,' the anthropologist said.

This fabricated malady signified a particular attitude – *if it's an illegitimate pregnancy, I will pretend not to see you* – that enabled the woman to carry through the pregnancy and abandon the baby when it was born. It also saved the mother from jail or execution when a corpse was found. I marvelled at this make-believe, head-in-the-sand disease that seemed a rich metaphor for so much. By declaring herself a 'bad mother' (with a defective uterus), the woman spared not only herself from punishment but also society from having to see its own failings: rapists getting off; their female victims being punished as though the only crime was theirs.

I felt uneasy for Ersilia, wondering if she was raped then told it was her fault for wearing her hair or blouse in a certain way, and whether it occurred to her to blame her bad uterus.

We had been talking for an hour, and the afternoon had grown colder and gloomier when the conversation shifted from more general matters regarding the history of the treatment of unmarried mothers in Bologna to Ersilia. I felt a surge of butterflies. Now perhaps I'd get some answers to help shed light on that burning question that had brought us to Bologna: why did she give up her daughter?

The anthropologist knew little of Ersilia's situation beyond what Milena had told her over email: that there was a midwife, a birth certificate, and she could afford the foundling home fee and cost of her baby's journey to Bologna. All of this, the anthropologist said, pointed towards Ersilia having a supportive family. Her baby could have been born out of a love story and not violent intercourse, which always resulted in the baby being abandoned with no papers. I was relieved for Ersilia; she was not a rape victim.

We now shared those other details we had learnt more recently about Ersilia's mature age, the illegitimate son, that her mother had died before the children were born, how they lived with her father, that she never married. With each new piece of information came subtle changes in the anthropologist's body language: an altered expression, stiffened shoulders, knowing 'Ah's.

I ignored them or failed to grasp the significance. Perhaps I was in denial – or else was caught up in the adrenaline rush of imagining I was on some investigative journalism assignment. This was the first day of what was meant to be an intensive week of interviews that would take Milena and my family across the Emilia-Romagna region. Irrespective of the reason, and despite my earlier suspicions about Ersilia's family, in this moment I was thinking like a reporter who's landed a hard-to-get interview and not as a descendent about to uncover an ugly secret. I had my newspaper correspondent's hat on and wanted to know what the anthropologist knew; I was greedy for her informed speculation.

I leant in across the table towards her, our co-conspirator in solving the mystery of Natalina's abandonment. 'How do you explain this?' I asked. 'Keeping her son …'

'It makes me scared, this here.' She looked over at my researcher uneasily. 'The presence of this father, with her having children.' She laughed nervously. 'It makes you think badly.'

'Yes, but in what sense?' Milena asked. 'Because it could be …' Her voice trailed off.

I agonised over the writing of what follows, given that the anthropologist's response was pure speculation. Repeating it here, I could be unfairly besmirching long-dead relatives, not to mention upsetting living ones. As a theory, it may be entirely wrong. Indeed, we would come into further information after the interview that would cause me to doubt its veracity. Yet I have chosen to include it because without it, Ersilia's story is incomplete, my retelling of it dishonest.

'*Incesto*,' said the anthropologist.

'Incest?' I spluttered. No need to translate that word.

Her voice softened as she explained incest was widespread, the norm, that it wasn't even seen as a bad thing. Incest as a concept didn't exist until the end of the nineteenth century and only in the city, not the countryside, which was behind.

I reeled but outwardly held it together, admitting that the possibility had crossed my mind, though I'd never mentioned it to anyone before (hoping if I didn't say it out loud, it wouldn't be true – kind of like the *madrazza*). It was only when the anthropologist suggested something else, that Natalina's abandonment 'could have been an act of protection', that the full significance of what she was saying hit home.

It felt like my brain was being squeezed and I held my forehead. 'By whom?'

'It could have been an act of protection on behalf of the mother to give the girl away, to protect the baby.'

My stomach churned. 'From what?'

The anthropologist looked nervously from me to Milena. 'From the father.'

'Her *own* father?' I cried, incredulous. 'Who would have abused her *daughter*?'

'If it was a case of–'

'Oh my God.'

I felt stunned, like I had been knocked to the floor. I had just been offered a possible answer to the mystery I so desperately wanted to solve, but every part of me recoiled from it. I wished I was anywhere but sitting on that terrace, fenced in by those metal balcony railings. Was this my family, was this what had made me? It was as though in that moment Ersilia's shame had transferred onto me, her descendent, four generations later. I wore it like a monk's hairshirt; it scratched and rubbed against my skin and I wanted to tear it off in anger and lob it back at the anthropologist.

Exactly *how* common was incest in the countryside at the time? I asked. She replied, gently, that she couldn't say; these things were hidden, very hidden; Bologna was a city once governed by the pope. I told her it was a terrible thing to imagine ('suggest', I wanted to say), that I would never be able to speak about any of this to my family.

The woman tried to soothe me, telling me it was a hypothesis, not the 'truth', that there were many other possible scenarios. Perhaps Ersilia had a fiancé but couldn't go through with the wedding because she had to help her father or lacked the financial means to assemble a dowry.

Maybe it wasn't Ersilia's father, but a member of the wider family, a cousin, an uncle – oftentimes many generations lived together. But then Milena mentioned Ersilia's miscarriages and the anthropologist sighed.

'The poor woman,' she said, and my heart sank.

This was a difficult history, she counselled. I had to look for the mother's love, which was evident here: Ersilia took care with the birth, she had the baby at home with a midwife; she entrusted Natalina to the institution she knew would care for her, would guarantee her milk, medical care and – critically – a dowry.

All of Bologna's female foundlings were entitled to one; without it, they would be unlikely to ever find a husband. Mothers abandoning their daughters factored this into their decision-making. The Bastardini hospital cut off payments to foster families when foundlings turned fifteen and for boys this was the end; they had to fend for themselves. But for girls, the institution continued to behave like a father, responsible for their honour, by giving them the possibility of marrying one day. The dowry would have comprised mostly household items – sheets, tablecloths, curtains – plus money; things that, along with her virtue, made a foundling an attractive prospect for a single man of limited means. If female foundlings did not marry, they could return to the Bastardini to live out their days, working for their food and lodging by making textiles. Only when girls were legitimised through marriage, or became nuns, did they cease to belong to the foundling home.

Ersilia probably knew all this: her act may have been selfless.

Still, I would not be mollified. I countered that although it was reassuring to believe that Ersilia wanted to protect her daughter, three out of four babies left at the foundling home in Natalina's situation ultimately perished. Wasn't consigning one's baby to the Bastardini hospital more like a death sentence? Then I put to the anthropologist that awful presumption I'd made about women like Ersilia: had she ever come across mothers who didn't love their abandoned children?

'No.' In all her research, she had never encountered a case of a mother abandoning a child where there was no love at all. Maybe a lack of understanding, but never the absence of love.

'Breathe in the air of San Giovanni, the big Bolognese countryside,' she told me. 'Try to think of how much this mother loved that baby she abandoned. Think of it like that. As a love story.'

Why was it so hard for me to do that? What prevented me from believing Ersilia acted out of love in removing her daughter from a situation where she might have been in danger, in giving her the chance of one day having the family that she never had herself? Even as I was told this woman was possibly raped by her own father, I wanted to quibble over statistics. What did I expect this mother with no other options but the foundling home to do?

We talked about other things with the anthropologist that day. I asked, for example, whether attitudes towards unmarried pregnant women softened by the close of the nineteenth century and her answer surprised me. To the contrary, she replied. The beginning of the twentieth century signalled a repositioning of women: the start of the idea of the woman's guilt, of blaming her for the pregnancy, the notion that even if she was raped, it was her fault. Before then, such women were considered poor, desperate, unlucky.

'The closer you get to 1900 the more doubt there is that perhaps she wanted it, she asked for it. I've never found this idea of it being the woman's fault, for attracting the man who raped her, in the trial notes from the 1800s.'

Time and again I would hear this during my research in Bologna: that in rape cases it was always the woman who provoked, not the male who violated.

While the bizarre *madrazza* diagnosis disappeared sometime in the twentieth century, the dissembling and hypocrisy did not. For instance, abortion was common in Italy by the early 1970s but it was not legalised until 1978. And today, though it is a right, for many women it is almost impossible to obtain one with an increase in the number of doctors – who can conscientiously object – unwilling to perform them.

'The way you see things, the way you are seen culturally and socially, has a continuity with the past,' said the anthropologist. 'Maybe the words change.'

It was 2018 when I sat down with the anthropologist on the terrace. Ireland, another fiercely Catholic country, had just voted by referendum to lift the prohibition on abortion. Previously, Irish women had to travel abroad to access the procedure; the death by sepsis of a woman who'd suffered a miscarriage and was denied an abortion was instrumental in convincing voters to approve the constitutional amendment. Back then it seemed Ireland was dragging the chain. Legal abortion arrived much sooner in Italy partly because World War II, with the absence of so many men from the home front, had transformed the place of women in society. With developments in Ireland, it felt – erroneously – like the death knell was sounding to the influence of religion over this aspect of social policy in the Western world.

Then came the overturning of *Roe v Wade*. The US Supreme Court would not get the conservative Christian majority required to bring about such a seismic change until late 2020, with President Donald Trump's third judicial appointment. The Court's decision two years later in *Dobbs v Jackson Women's Health Organization* was a heart-stopping moment when it wound the clock back disastrously on the rights of women to choose whether to become mothers. The Court's reasoning – that the US Constitution said nothing about abortion and therefore such rights could not be implicitly guaranteed – was breathtakingly brazen given that the founding document was written by men in 1787, a time when women could not vote, hold political office or become judges.

In multiple US states, abortion is a crime once again, with no exceptions for rape or incest. I felt foolish to have been shocked at the surveillance of pregnant women in nineteenth-century Bologna, who were treated as outlaws and imprisoned until their babies were born. I thought I had been dealing with an anachronism, but these things are happening in current-day America.

The only time I feared an unwanted pregnancy, as a single professional in my late twenties, I purchased a morning-after pill from the chemist without giving it a second thought. It was outside my experience to know what it would have been like for Ersilia to be confronted with an unwanted pregnancy and to have no option but to go through with it. Knowing she would not be able to keep the child when it was born, whether for poverty or some other reason.

I tried to imagine her. A poor, single, uneducated woman living in a rural town, supporting her father and son. There was never enough to eat. I saw her rise early, before the sun, pull her pinafore over her head, tuck her hair into a skullcap, take her apron and set out for her workplace. The only job available to her was in domestic service, working in the house of a wealthy family where she was vulnerable to an unscrupulous boss. Was the man attentive at first? Did he compliment her large, round, heavy-lidded eyes, then lure her into a darkened room when her mistress was not around? Or did he force himself onto her, rough and brutal, tearing her undergarments and leaving her bleeding in the shed with the animals? Perhaps it wasn't her boss at all, but her boyfriend, the young man who had promised to marry her but then reneged and, once she was pregnant, didn't want to know her. Or perhaps it was someone else, someone even more familiar to her ... Oh, the humiliation, the disgrace, the horror, the overwhelm.

In trying to connect with the experiences of nineteenth-century Italian women like Ersilia, I thought back to the times when, as a girl and a young woman, I felt threatened. Several incidents came to mind, uneasy moments, lucky escapes. They were nothing like what she would have faced, but I was constructing a bridge across time and space to my ancestor, attempting to go beyond the anthropological studies, to take what I had learnt and breathe life into her past. Our lives were separated by a century, but we had in common the fear of sexual violence that comes with inhabiting a woman's body, in any period.

I remembered the older boy who used to follow me home from the bus stop in my early years of high school. When I saw him – the grey shirt, grey shorts, ratty schoolbag slung over one shoulder – a chill would spread through my body. My throat would dry up and I'd become voiceless. The only sound was the thumping of my heart as the rest of the world disappeared. All I could see was that moon face covered in dark, overlapping freckles, that wolfish smile as the uninvited arm reached around my back and he pressed his head close to mine. The boy ignored my protests, never questioned his right to violate me in this way. I dreaded and feared those afternoons. The walk home was only two streets, but it felt like kilometres. I'd pray as I stepped off the bus that he was sick that day and wouldn't be there, waiting for me. I changed bus stops for a while, walked the longer route home, up a steep hill. I made up stories, told him my father was a policeman and would come looking for him. While it was happening, for reasons I do not recall – other than perhaps I was embarrassed, ashamed – I told no-one about it.

Then there was the young Italian motorcyclist I met at a New Year's Eve party in Trieste when I was nineteen, who invited me out. As we were walking the dark streets of the unfamiliar city, he asked why I had agreed to go out with him when he could be a serial killer. I fled in a passing taxi.

The man at a pedestrian signal crossing in Sydney's CBD who whacked me over the head with a plastic shopping bag. The bag contained a wooden box filled with beads that spilled out all over George Street. I was on my way to the part-time job I held during my law school days. Afterwards I recounted the incident in a letter to a friend, writing that I ran into the nearby Grace Bros department store and that '*nobody* asked me if I was okay'.

There were the months I lived in London's East End in my mid-twenties. More than once I sprinted home from the tube station after work because I feared a man was trailing me.

The time as a journalist in my early thirties when I asked my boyfriend (now husband) to come to the National Press Club, where I was meeting a political staffer for a drink after work – it was part of the job – because I didn't feel safe being alone with him.

Another incident has stayed with me. I was in Brussels on a program for visiting media when an interview subject invited me to a bar with his friends (male and female). I had nothing else to do that night, knowing no-one else in that city. We danced, he plied me with alcohol then drove me back to my hotel, where I let him come inside my room for 'one last drink'. I sobered up quickly when I realised his intentions were different to mine. I became frightened that if I told him I didn't want to have sex with him he might get angry, and I would be overpowered. It was only by letting him kiss me, then promising to meet the following night – by implying he would get what he wanted then – that I was able to make him leave. I did not see him again.

When the anthropologist left, I sent the Italian teacher home too. Afterwards, Milena stood with me on the terrace while I supported myself against the table, unable to speak. This compassionate young woman with curly hair and a wide smile, whom I'd only just met in person for the first time that morning – all our earlier communication having been on email – tried to console me.

'This is Natalina's story,' she said, gently stroking my arm. 'Why do you feel so bad?'

Silence.

'Is it revulsion at what happened to Ersilia, or what it means for you?'

I could not answer her, though it was primarily the latter. Faced with the tragedy of Ersilia's possible abuse, the truth was I thought only of myself. What it meant for me was that a part of my identity I celebrated – my Italian heritage – had turned bad. I didn't want to learn any more Italian. I didn't want to know anything else about Ersilia. I wanted to run as far away as possible from her story, but couldn't now, because it was inside me.

I thought of Oedipus, abandoned by his father to avoid fulfilling a dark prophecy, who unwittingly married his mother. I understood his impulse to blind himself with pins from his wife's dress upon learning the truth, so he wouldn't have to see. I had disturbed a history that should have been left to lie. Had taken the past and made it present. Now I shouldered the burden of that knowledge as no generation since had done – not Natalina, nor her daughters. I had allowed my obsession with a dead woman to sully our living family, to touch my son.

In my notebook I scrawled: 'I can't write this, can't tell anyone, can't let my mother listen to the interview, can't tell my siblings.' My instinct told me to bury it, though I knew I couldn't: 'This is a story you wish you'd left alone, wish you'd never uncovered, but now you have to live with it.'

I wondered if the bad things that had happened to me were punishment for something my ancestors did. That passage in the Old Testament came to mind: 'I will not fail to punish children and grandchildren to the third and fourth generation for the sins of their parents.' Was it a coincidence that, exactly 120 years after Natalina's birth, it was me who had dug up the name of the woman who abandoned her? That I had uncovered her dreadful story?

'Suffering feels like punishment,' writes historian Elaine Pagels. She links this to Genesis and the teaching that sin was a choice – Eve's – and that it caused the perfect world God created to go bad, bringing on all the torments we have suffered ever since. The idea that innocent children should be punished for what their fathers did four generations ago played to some of my darkest, most warped, Catholic-inspired fears.

My thoughts turned to our lonely child, who was spending too much time on the iPad. I chastised myself for bringing him to Bologna. I would set up a playdate with our Italian teacher's boys; that's what I would do. In the meantime, using a recipe Valentina gave me for a simple tuna and tomato spaghetti, I cooked his dinner on the stove that was too high for me (sitting in the wheelchair, I could not see into the pot to stir it). He refused to eat it. Then I went to bed with a blinding headache, on the too-soft futon that was giving me debilitating back pain.

Over the course of my research in Bologna, new details would come to light about Ersilia's situation. The director of the Archivio Storico Provinciale, while not dismissing the possibility that incest played a role in her conception, would tell me the actual circumstances could be 'so many and so different'. Ersilia might have lived with her father because she had no other option. She might have had a relationship with a man who never married her, and so she kept the first child because her father allowed her to and helped her raise it, but he couldn't do this with the second. It could have been a case of 'simple poverty, ignorance'.

I would also obtain Paolino's official birth certificate. Signed by Ersilia, it stated the boy's father was an unmarried man, unrelated to her, and that their relationship was not of sufficient consequence to justify his recognition of their child. Unrelated. *Non parente*. Still, I couldn't help but wonder: would Ersilia have told the truth on her son's birth certificate if his father *was* related to her?

Midway through our trip, my parents joined us. I relayed some, though not all, of my findings about Natalina to my mother. We were sitting in a café in Trieste. Not once did I mention the 'i' word, wanting to protect her from the anthropologist's theories. My mother listened with mild interest, before casually observing, 'Maybe Natalina is a child of incest. In those days you kept it hidden.' After picking my jaw up off the table, I pondered my fear and shame when such a possibility hadn't rattled her at all.

5
Perspectives

Buying a scooter was the Italian teacher's idea. All week our little boy had been trailing us around the city, visiting churches, archives, libraries, museums. His legs were tired, he complained, could he climb onto the wheelchair with me? 'Please, Mamma?' He had done it as a baby, then as a toddler, and I loved that he still wanted to sit with me – even if only because he was tired.

This was his 'normal'. A mother in a self-propelled chair, a mother with removable legs. A mother too scared to take her child out by herself in a foreign city in case something went wrong. Not for hot chocolate, not to buy him new shoes, not to search for sliced bread that didn't crumble in your hands when you tried to butter it.

In Bologna, every time we encountered a difficult section of footpath or road, Michael would take the handles of my wheelchair – it was a routine we were used to – and push me. I was grateful to have such a selfless, loving husband who was always looking out for me. Even so, I sometimes felt like an infant in a pram. How did my son see me, I wondered, that I required looking after in this way?

'I wish I could do magic and make you walk again, Mum,' L said once. 'But even without your legs you are still the best mum in the world.'

It breaks your heart then patches it back together, all in the same breath.

As a child, nothing was as exciting as accompanying my mother on shopping expeditions. Hanging off that overloaded supermarket trolley with errant wheels as she steered it through Franklins doing our weekly grocery shop was my idea of heaven. It saddened me that I could never re-create these experiences for my son with the same freedom, autonomy and regularity as my mother. Boarding a bus every other Saturday with four ratty children and setting off for an afternoon exploring a multi-level Westfields shopping mall – another favourite pastime – was simply out of the question for me.

When my son was little, however, sitting together on the wheelchair – even just to explore our house – offered consolation. Something that came close to replicating the feelings I had during those shopping trips with my mother. It was an intimate, shared experience that was unique to us. When we were nestled this way, my child resting his back into me, so close I'd inhale his freshly shampooed hair, his little boy scent, we encountered the world together. It also reminded me of those surreal final weeks of the pregnancy when our bodies were as one; when resting my hand on my large, stretched belly, I rested on him too.

Fast-forward and it was all very congenial travelling this way under the smooth porticoes. Every time we met with a bumpy cobblestoned laneway, however, I feared the wheelchair was going to crack under the weight of us.

Our Italian teacher was always thinking of ways to enrich our son's time in her city. Knowing his affection for trains, Valentina once cut out a picture of a locomotive to teach him the days of the week; each carriage was a different day. But he ran off with it into another room, making 'ding ding' noises like a Melbourne tram, and refused to come back. After that she decided the best way to engage him was to organise excursions for us around the city. Some highlights: the mortadella room at the Museo della Storia di Bologna, the red tourist train to the Santuario della Madonna di San Luca, the largest LEGO city in the world at the deconsecrated San Mattia church (still a place of worship, but a new god had moved in).

Her pupil might enjoy his time better in Bologna with its 60 kilometres of porticoes, she gently told me following one of our lessons, if he had his own set of wheels. 'You could get him a scooter.'

It was an appealing idea, but I was unsure it would work. Was it safe? Would the Bolognese mind our son riding their medieval porticoes on a scooter? Would we get disapproving glances or worse? It seemed a little extravagant as he already had one back in Australia. Where would we buy one in this city unfit for children? With three young boys of her own, Valentina knew just the place.

The day of the scooter purchase was inhospitably cold, grey, drizzly. I had hired a guide to take us on a walking tour of Bologna and, as we set off to meet her, visiting the scooter shop wasn't part of the plan. We met outside the twelfth-century Palazzo D'Accursio, once the house of the papal legate and now the municipal palace, in Piazza Maggiore. My hope was that, as an employee of the city's official tourist bureau, a guide would be able to sneak us into the Bastardini hospital.

Elena arrived in skinny jeans and white sneakers. She was young, had commuted in from Modena, an hour's drive away, and did not – it was clear from the start – possess the keys to the medieval city.

Nursing my disappointment as we toured various other landmarks instead, I noticed that whenever Elena opened her mouth to describe some historical artefact, L would start to grizzle. Not too loud, but enough so we had to strain to hear. Approaching our final destination of Santo Stefano, Bologna's most sacred quarter, our whining son had reached his limit. I read it in his weary face and slumped shoulders. Enough with the staircases built for horses; the martyrs carrying their decapitated heads; the open-air mausoleums encasing dead medieval law professors!

'Just one more stop,' I pleaded with him.

Santo Stefano was a mystical complex of ancient churches. This was where Bologna's pregnant women and prostitutes once came to pray: in a fifth-century basilica built on the ruins of a pagan temple above a natural spring. The temple had been erected to Isis, Egyptian goddess of healing and protector of women and children. Inside the millennia-old basilica, the air was cool and damp and made my skin prickle, as though electrically charged. That entwinement of Christian and pre-Christian deities appealed to me; so too the idea that the women were drawn to forces more primal than ones the men in charge would have ever wanted to acknowledge.

Exiting, I noticed L staring forlornly into the bottom of the raised well in Santo Stefano's central cloistered courtyard and felt the twinge of mean mother guilt. That clinched it. I announced that a visit to Città del Sole, 'Sun City', the local toy shop, was in order.

Our son's eyes lit up when he spied the red Maxi Micro. The scooter was little, like him. It had a bright red deck and grips and three wheels, and was perfect for careening along the smooth pavements beneath the porticoes. Outside the shop, in a darkened medieval laneway behind Bologna's Asinelli and Garisenda towers, he posed contentedly with his *monopattino* and matching red helmet for a photo.

He was now a different child to the one who, days before, I'd overheard talking to the stuffed toys he'd brought from home. We had just banned him from playing with his Hot Wheels cars on the apartment floor in case he scratched the timber boards. They were all prisoners, he informed Chino the dinosaur, Tatty the bear and the rest, and the barred door to the terrace was the door of their jail cell.

The little red scooter proved a master stroke. It gave L a sense of autonomy in an alien city I had forced upon him, in turn allowing me to feel more at home with my wheelchair in the land of my maternal ancestors, where I yearned to fit in. We could now ride Bologna's porticoes together.

Following the trail of women in extremis led us, another day, to Palazzo Poggi, the current-day seat of the University of Bologna. I had read about the Museum of Obstetrics housed there, with its collection of wax models and birthing machines designed to educate doctors and midwives in the eighteenth century. Amid the startling cabinets of women's uteruses, the fetuses with an array of imperfections – hare lips, single eyes, all believed at the time to be caused by the emotions of women disgusted with their pregnancies – was a story I was not expecting.

Anna Morandi Manzolini was a female anatomist extraordinaire during Enlightenment Bologna. Born around 1714, Morandi met her husband, a wax modeller and anatomist, while studying sculpture and drawing. When he died unexpectedly, leaving her with two young children, she took over the studio where they had previously worked together dissecting cadavers and creating eerily realistic wax models for surgeons and medical students.

Despite her own international renown, Morandi struggled financially as a single parent. The Senate of Bologna awarded her an annual honorarium for her work as public modeller and lecturer of anatomy at the University of Bologna, but it was not enough to support herself and her two children. Consequently, she placed one of them, the eldest, twelve-year-old Giuseppe, into an orphanage.

Learning this, I felt that impulse to judge, focusing on the child's loss – how could she do it to him? – rather than on the constraints the mother found herself in. On her sacrifice. On the outcome. She made a choice, as Ersilia did. Except Morandi kept the youngest child, perhaps believing he needed her more.

Ultimately, the elder son was adopted by an aristocratic family who wanted an heir, while Morandi, from a poor background and with no formal degree, grew in skill and reputation to be considered the best anatomist of her day. Her special interests were the sense organs (eyes, ears, nose, tongue, hands) and – unheard of for a woman – the male reproductive system. When she died in 1774 her sons, together, purchased an enormous gravestone and she was buried in the nave of the San Procolo church, across the road from the Bastardini foundling home.

It was as though I had a vision deficiency that caused me to view all mothers with a yellow tinge, like the light that first night in Bologna. Yellow also being the colour of judgement. Morandi, on the other hand, saw herself very clearly, with obvious pride in both her womanliness and her professional achievements. I surmise this because she left behind a telling self-portrait: a wax figure dressed in ultra-feminine garb of taffeta, lace and pearls, with perfectly curled (real) hair, her hands poised to dissect the human brain in front of her, her face with the hint of a smile.

After the speculation on the terrace, I was about as excited for more historical family research as our son was. But the archivists at the Archivio Storico Provinciale were expecting me and so, a couple of days later, we set out for the institute. It was inside the southwestern Porta Saragozza gate, in a building on the edge of a weedy car park overshadowed by linden trees. From the outside it looked like a modern guard house set into a brick perimeter wall. We pressed the intercom then the softly spoken director, Dr Letizia Bongiovanni, draped in a snakeskin print scarf, and her affable, bespectacled offsider, Dr Francesco Rosa, ushered us inside.

Dr Bongiovanni presided over foundling home artefacts that dated back to 1417. They included, in addition to the files of abandoned babies, the *medagliere*, the medal collection. I had read about how mothers sometimes left half medallions with their babies when they relinquished them to the foundling home, hiding the fragments inside their swaddling. Mothers did this in case they ever returned to claim their child – though this rarely happened in practice. The medals were mainly religious: crosses and other sacred images. Producing the token would provide proof of identity, evidence of the woman's claim to motherhood, with the mother having kept the other half.

I wanted to see these medallions with my own eyes. These fragments bound mother and baby; they were an unspoken promise, whispered across the ages. The act of splitting those medals in two, while conveying the painful break of the maternal bond, gave permission to hope, holding out the possibility that the whole might be reassembled one day, mother and child rejoined.

I imagined the bated breath when the mother turned up unannounced at the doors of the Bastardini hospital, presenting her part of the medallion and asking for her child back. The rapture when the two halves were matched, and the reunion the child never stopped believing in eventuated. The long wait coming to a fairytale end. In a system designed to irreparably sever the bond between the unwed mother and her child, the thought of foundling home officials searching the newly arrived babies' swaddling for their mothers' trinkets, then safeguarding them in perpetuity, surprised me. It came across as a chink of humanity in a process that seemed otherwise devoid of it.

With so few mothers ever actually returning, however, the broken medallions could also be seen as broken promises. In any event, my great-grandmother was denied even the faintest chance of this happening since her mother never left her with anything. When Bastardini officials unwrapped baby Natalina that evening after the midwife had surrendered her, they found no concealed keepsake. The lack of any *contrassegno*, identifying symbol, was noted on her birth record. I wondered what this meant, that Ersilia had left not even the tiniest shred of herself with her daughter. Was her child so unwanted?

The archivists led me to a freestanding timber wardrobe. The oddly placed closet had already caught my eye. In a room that was otherwise bland – white walls, white floor tiles, laminated tables, grey chairs – the wardrobe stood out. It was pushed up against the wall, opposite a photocopier and trolleys stacked with books. In front of it, a few readers sat quietly hunched over files, deep in concentration. Beside it, light spilled into the room through a door and window overlooking a garden. Large and unadorned, the wardrobe stood there alone, locked up and unassuming, betraying nothing of its contents. Certainly not the fact that, like the famous cabinet of C.S. Lewis's imagination, it contained a passageway to another world.

As I waited for the archivists to locate the key to the wardrobe, I recalled my own medallion given to me by my nonna, who arranged for her sister-in-law to bring it out from Italy when I was born. It was triangular, gold, the size of a fingernail, with an engraving of the Virgin Mary cradling the baby Jesus. My mother says giving a medallion is an Italian custom, one she has carried on with her own grandchildren. I still wear mine on a necklace.

Dr Bongiovanni turned the key and prised opened the doors, explaining that the armoire was brought over from the foundling home and was in its original condition. As the doors yawned open, I felt the breath catch in my chest. Inside was a wall of broken medallions, over a thousand of them, lined up in rows by year. The mothers' mementoes were organised the same way they had been from 1776 until 1898 – coincidentally, the year Natalina was born. Each one was attached to a square paper containing a name, date of birth and number. The squares hung from nails driven into the back panel of the shallow wardrobe, with a nail for every year, written in red on a separate piece of white paper. I counted seventeen rows across, eight columns down. There were Madonnas, crucifixes, coins, rosaries, earrings, coral bracelets, beads, ribbons, folds of fabric, chains, playing cards, prayer cards, pouches embroidered with names, a pin cushion in the shape of a heart. Everything a half.

The crude timber backboard was pockmarked with white stains, as though someone had tried to fill holes with putty; possibly, it was mould. Large envelopes lined the floor of the wardrobe. They were filled with tokens from the years when officials stopped pinning them up.

Many of the squares of paper containing the babies' information, I noticed, were inscribed at the bottom with a tiny black cross. Along the top row of nails, for example, I counted nine crosses – more than half. Dr Bongiovanni told me if the square was marked with a cross, it meant the baby died in the foundling home. The number of crosses was prodigious, transforming the closet into a kind of columbarium.

'It was a period of infant mortality that today we can't comprehend,' she said in Italian.

I thought of the mortality rate the year Natalina was born: three-quarters of babies without mothers to feed them, dead. Seeing the crosses beneath those babies' names, literally tethered to their mother's remains in the form of the half medallion, brought the numbers to life. How many of those mothers ever knew their babies had died?

The enormity of the loss was further underscored when, afterwards, Dr Rosa produced the wet-nurse register from Natalina's birth year. We located Natalina's individual page in the enormous linen-covered book. She was foundling number 521 in 1898. I drew my eyes across the scribblings that marked out her life. There were names, numbers, addresses and notes in red, blue and black ink, documenting major milestones, beginning with her birth and ending in her marriage.

I looked through the entries before and after hers. These pages were blank, save for the names of each baby, the wet nurse they were assigned to at the top, and the tell-tale cross. On one such page it was noted that a salary had been paid for one year to a wet nurse after she contracted syphilis from the now-dead baby. Natalina was sandwiched between two children who did not live.

Peering into that wardrobe was like taking the lid off an ancient jar filled with mothers' tears. The smell of grief hit me hard. It was like the mothers' hurt had leached into each object. It was the jolt I needed to finally start appreciating those mothers as real women faced with impossible choices. Women who didn't want to give away the babies they'd carried for nine months, feeling the alien kicks inside their bellies, wondering about the unborn child's sex, the colour of their eyes, skin, hair, the shape of their mouth. Women who felt they had no other option. The broken medallions gave those nameless mothers a story: of the pain each one must have felt the day she cut that piece of ribbon, tore that red playing card, snapped that metal disc in two.

It was a shock to be confronted so viscerally with this image of those women using these precious artefacts to mark their babies as their own, even as they were giving them away. At last, I saw the mother's love that I hadn't been able to before. Love constrained by circumstance. The medallions represented more than broken promises; they were also broken hearts.

I asked the archivists what they made of the absence of a token for Natalina. Dr Bongiovanni told me that because her mother left no '*segni di riconoscimento*', no sign of recognition, her act of abandonment was strong. She said, 'From what we know, the only thing we can say is that this woman didn't think she was capable of raising her own daughter and she gave it away decisively.'

She explained that it was usually married mothers who left markers of identification. They had husbands, sometimes older children, and may have been too poor to keep another infant. Their married status allowed them to hope that, if ever their family found its way out of poverty, they could reclaim their abandoned children. But Natalina's mother was in a different position. Unmarried Ersilia may have left no half medallion because, tied to her elderly father, and already bringing up an illegitimate son, she could not conceive of any improvement in her circumstances that would ever allow her to reclaim her second child.

Ersilia had no intention of returning for Natalina; that was clear. Looking in the wardrobe, however, I understood this did not mean that she suffered any less than the mothers who left tokens. If anything, being completely without hope, she may have suffered more. I thought of a line in Hans Christian Andersen's fairytale *The Little Mermaid*, 'it seemed as if she must have wept, but a mermaid has no tears, and that makes her suffer all the more'. I saw it now. The absence of a token did not signify that her love for her abandoned child was any less; it simply pointed to the fact that her constraints were greater.

I asked to see the last keepsake from 1898 anyway. It was a half metal disc, attached to a piece of white ribbon. It did not belong to Natalina. I stepped back and Dr Bongiovanni locked the cupboard again.

Getting around in a wheelchair makes you see places differently; getting around in a wheelchair with a young child in tow offers another perspective yet again. When I think of Bologna now, I don't remember the lumpy cobblestones. Rather, I recall the porticoes with smooth, stone walkways the colour of speckled pink mortadella, which were superb for wheelchairs and zippy red scooters.

(The porticoes were built from the 1100s onwards to increase living spaces in crowded medieval Bologna; they supported the expanded upper floors of buildings and had to be not only publicly accessible but tall enough to fit a rider on a horse.)

I see the three of us in our black puffer jackets, my son and I riding side by side under the porticoes, Michael bringing up the rear. Huge smiles are plastered on our faces, as we head south through the crisp morning air towards Giardini Margherita, Bologna's major park.

(We whizz past a mini-mart, a home furnishing store, a shuttered tavern; then a motorbike passes us, vrooming and sputtering on the narrow, paved road.)

In that moment of joy, I am not thinking of that despised chair, of the many ways in which it limits my ability to care for my son. I am not thinking of what the Bolognese people make of us, the spectacle of a mother in a wheelchair racing her child on a scooter along their medieval porticoes.

(We slow for the zebra crossing, glance across to the arches on the other side of the road, see the façade of another uncompleted medieval church; then we're off again, my boy's little red helmet out in front, beside us the flash of pink and yellow and orange walls.)

Instead, as I spin those wheels with my arms, as L kicks his scooter along with his little legs, I am grounded in the present, thinking how wonderful it is to be in Bologna riding with my son, how lucky we are to be sharing this as a family. I am thinking of what the wheelchair gives us, that this is an experience only a child with a mother in one could know.

Still, there were times when I remembered the warnings of the naysayers that Italy was overly ambitious for someone like me, and wished I was back in my accessible house in Sydney. Occasions when I wondered why I had gone so out of my way to make the life I had even harder by insisting on it being a large life. Episodes which proved my fears that taking my son out by myself in an unfamiliar environment was beyond my abilities, unwise, too risky. Such as the time we toured a restored eleventh-century stone castle in Gorizia, outside Trieste.

The World War I battles of the Isonzo were fought here, on the eastern sector of the Italian Front. Ersilia's older boy, Paolino, was stationed somewhere close by from 1915 to 1918. Four years later, Natalina would move to nearby Trieste, some 30 kilometres away from where her brother, whose existence was unknown to her, had likely served.

It was a sunny day when we visited and, to our son's delight, snow lay melting on the grassy slopes that led up to the castle. When we reached the top of the hilltop fortification, just as we were about to enter the castle gates, L asked if he could remain outside. There was a sturdy-looking snowman that had not yet liquefied in the sun and he said he would rather play with that than tour yet another old castle. It seemed fair enough. I told my husband to go ahead without us. I can do this, I thought, securing the wheelchair brakes at the top of the slope.

As soon as Michael disappeared inside, L announced he needed the bathroom and that a tree wouldn't do. I peered up through the gates and saw a steep, uneven cobblestone path that twisted and turned around the castle walls and was impossible for a wheelchair. I looked down the hill. The paved pathway my husband had just pushed me up was long and precipitous, with a flowerbed on one side next to a retaining wall, and a staircase leading down into the gardens and the car park on the other. After more desperate whimpering from our son, I took a deep breath. My child needed me.

'It's okay, we'll go down the hill and find a toilet,' I said.

I unlocked the brakes and let the rubber rims of the wheelchair slip between my fingers. The wheelchair quickly picked up speed and I felt myself losing control. Realising I would do serious harm if I didn't stop, I swerved hard towards the muddy flowerbed and let the wheelchair tip me over into the vegetation. My leg twisted inside the prosthetic, and I cried out.

'It's my fault,' L sobbed, snowman forgotten.

'No, it's not.' I tried to pick myself up out of the flowerbed but couldn't get out of the ditch. So I sat up in the dirt and initiated a game of I-spy to distract him, praying Michael would return soon. I was angry, humiliated. This, I told myself, was mothering in a wheelchair. Disability stung my pride. The wheelchair didn't fit any aspect of the person I wanted to be: writer researching in a foreign land, capable mother of an active boy.

That was one bad experience among many positive ones. Early on after losing my legs I decided it was better to have half the experiences more physically able people enjoy than none at all. I couldn't climb the 498 stairs to the top of the Asinelli tower. But I could sit at the foot of its shorter, drifting neighbour, Garisenda, and read the plaque citing Dante Alighieri, who included a reference to the tower in his *Inferno*: 'just as the Garisenda tower, when viewed beneath its leaning side, appears to fall if any floating cloud should pass behind'. I could watch those floating clouds.

The thing is, in Bologna with its porticoes, I found a way to mother within the constraints that bound me, a new way to express my love for my son. The Italian teacher was right: he did enjoy the city much more with a scooter. It felt as though the porticoes were built for people like us: a family encumbered by daunting physical challenges, spurred on by even bigger dreams. When we eventually departed Italy, we left the trusty red scooter with my cousin, whose friend's young son was delighted to receive our gift.

6
Rupture

The only time I feared my mother would abandon me was when I was eight, and it wasn't an abandonment at all – she had merely gone into hospital to have my baby brother. It was 1980; I was in Year Three. Sister Pauline was my teacher. Small yet menacing, she was like an angry wombat in her brown habit and clumpy lace-up shoes. All day long she patrolled the rows of desks, on the lookout for signs we were not paying attention to her huge charts of times tables pinned up on the blackboard. Corporal punishment was an essential component of the school curriculum. It was either a stealthy whack across the arm for talking, or the cane across the hand for a more serious transgression. She once banned a boy from carrying a tote bag with an iron-on transfer of the American rock band Kiss because they played the devil's music. On the other hand, her methods worked and I've never forgotten my times tables.

Halfway through that unsettling year, my mother had her fourth and final child. One wintry night is marked indelibly on my brain. With Mum away in hospital, the rest of us hunkered down in the living room. The image is as fresh as yesterday. The stripey tan-and-gold sofa with matching armchairs. The dark green walls, which my mother was always painting different colours – there was never any white in our house. And a fire roaring in the black marble fireplace. My father loved open fires and would lug home gigantic, ant-infested logs from whatever bush site he happened to be surveying at the time. We were forever stamping out sparks in the carpet tiles.

Olivia Newton-John was on television that night performing Andrew Lloyd Webber's 'Don't Cry for me Argentina'. My father recorded it on an audio cassette and replayed it over and over afterwards. Hearing those lyrics that evening, about the truth being she never left them, without our mother there, made us children bawl. When I listen to that song now, with Eva Perón exhorting her people not to mourn her passing, I still feel a twist in my chest and remember the pain I felt listening to my father's recording. Life without my mother, I remember thinking, was not worth living.

The story of Ersilia and Natalina connects to a deeply held fear I harboured as a child – one that possibly every child has – of losing a parent. I carried it; our son, conscious of having older parents, carries it; Natalina lived it. The fear of the lost mother is deeply embedded in our family's history. One chilly day in Bologna, I discovered that this anxiety could be traced back even earlier to Ersilia's childhood, to a loss that upended her life and likely underpinned her daughter's abandonment.

We were at the Giardini Margherita. The 26-hectare park with its playgrounds and vast open spaces had become our son's happy place, the go-to destination for restoring his spirits when my research and homeschooling became too much. As it did one weekday when he refused to come out from under the bedcovers.

'No Mummy School,' he cried in a muffled voice.

I abandoned the morning's plans and suggested we take the Maxi Micro to the park instead. Recalling a disturbing dream I'd had the night before in which I was being pecked by a flock of colourful birds, I wrote in my journal: 'Today, I am not going to judge myself.'

That morning Bologna had just received its first dusting of snow. The air was damp and icy when we stopped in Piazza Maggiore to watch workmen with aerial cranes and cherry pickers dress the city's Christmas tree. We then continued along the endless porticoes, eventually finding the park gates and going in.

Enormous silvery cedars with weeping branches, pines and cypress trees overshadowed us. Although you could hear the low hum of traffic in the distance, inside the gardens the air was still and calming. The park was created in 1879 on the site of an old convent on the other side of the city's southern walls. Sometimes, I'd read, the nuns who ran the elementary school at the Bastardini hospital would take the foundlings there to play, marching them in single file through the city.

L spotted the play equipment and looked over at me. Should he kick the ball or play on the swing? Watching him charge about in his blue trackpants and grey jumper with a colourful star on the front, I thought of Ersilia and fished out my journal again.

> Ersilia, I'm sitting here in the old park in Bologna and it's the happiest my son has been all week. I'm here for selfish reasons, to comprehend why you did what you did. I'm exhausted, I feel guilty being here, but I'm trying to understand.

Could she hear me? Did my words rouse her spirit? I wanted her to know I was there. I wanted her to know that I saw her.

The gardens were filled with joggers, couples, men pushing prams, youths, dog walkers, a woman cycling, a man smoking in the middle of a green field. I studied the fallen seed pods, the tree trunks encrusted with lichen. Birds twittered: tits, wagtails, sparrows, swifts?

My phone beeped. A WhatsApp message informed me a letter had arrived from San Giovanni in Persiceto with new information regarding Ersilia's childhood. I stared at the screen and thought of that journal entry. Was it a coincidence that she chose to reveal herself today, in Giardini Margherita?

According to the letter, Ersilia came from a much larger family than the one I had initially found living at Via Abate when her daughter was born. In 1866, the year the civil registry was established in the new Italian state, when Ersilia was one, three generations of the Serra family lived under one roof on Strada Samoggia in the rural parish of San Giacomo del Martignone in the municipality of Anzola dell'Emilia. This included her paternal grandmother, her parents, Teodoro and Enrica, an older brother, Enrico, and an older sister, Ernesta. When she was four her younger sister, Argia, was born (her parents must have exhausted all 'E' names by then). Later, there came another brother.

Her father was one of the *braccianti*, wage labourers, a rising work force in industrialising Italy with one of the lowest social standings. As such he had no regular employment and, unlike sharecroppers, was forced to find his own accommodation. This was usually cramped, unhygienic lodgings in a rural town centre. The family's house belonged to the local doctor. It would have been small, poorly made of stone or brick, with glassless windows, no ceiling and a dirt floor. It was possible the family moved to other houses: agricultural workers such as Teodoro typically moved every year in search of seasonal work. But the family always remained in the same parish – until tragedy struck.

Teodoro's livelihood, hemp, was an important industry in the Bologna region; in fact, it was so lucrative that laws protected knowledge of the manufacturing process. All kinds of items were made from hemp: underwear, textiles for the house, linen, cords. At one time the Venetians used Bologna's high-quality hemp to make sails for their ships.

Hemp work was gruelling, considered by many a punishment from God. Every day Teodoro would have gathered with other workers in the central piazza, hoping to be selected by a boss for a day's labour. The dark green hemp stalks, sown in spring, grew to 4 or 5 metres. Under the merciless August sun, peasant workers cut the stems with a scythe or sickle and wrangled them into large bundles, working from dawn to dusk. They beat them on the ground to remove the leaves, dried them, then placed the bundles into water under large stones to macerate. Once the woody part of the stem had detached from the inner fibres, the workers hauled them out, wet and even heavier than before. Hours were spent trudging waist-deep in streams or ponds where conditions were stiflingly humid, mosquitoes were unrelenting – malaria was rife – and the stench was overpowering and stupefying. In one account I read, hemp workers likened the ordeal to Jesus Christ in the Garden of Gethsemane, begging his father to 'let this cup pass from me'.

Ersilia's brother Enrico would have accompanied their father to the hemp fields from a young age; probably their mother did too. I wonder if Ersilia wished she could join them or whether the tall, dark hemp forests frightened her. She would have heard stories about the monsters who lurked inside, lying in wait for a child to become lost or separated from the others.

Instead, Ersilia's days would have been spent assisting her nonna around the house, along with her sister: folding away the beds, sweeping the dirt floor, feeding the chickens, foraging for brushwood, helping prepare the cabbage *minestra* that would simmer for hours in the heavy copper cauldron in time for her father's return. (If there was ever egg or meat to be had, it was saved for Teodoro.) School attendance would have been irregular, though Enrica may well have encouraged her daughters to go after the village employed a female teacher. Ersilia could read and write.

San Giacomo was located on the swampy Samoggia flood plain. This was also where Ersilia's parents were born, on the Terre d'Acqua or 'Water Lands'. It was said the people there lived suspended between earth and water. I pictured some mythological creature, part human, part frog, who could thrive in both habitats – like the peasants in Ovid's *Metamorphosis* with their ill-natured croakings, 'seized with a desire to plunge beneath the water'. But the dwellers of the plain were not amphibious in this pure sense. The river was a bountiful resource they depended on for their livelihoods, yet it could also be a destabilising threat that stymied human settlement for centuries. Locals said the river, when it burst its banks, was like a beast scraping away at the plain in search of a new place to live.

The family's district was criss-crossed by torrents and streams, of which the Samoggia was the most important. The river ran parallel to the family's street. Back then, before the river's banks were raised and it was dammed in the twentieth century, its waters were clean enough to drink and teemed with life: goldfish swam in the shallows, and catfish, carp, doctor fish, pike and eels in the depths. The grasses and reeds hummed with insects and thudding frogs. Birdlife was abundant – moorhens, ducks, snipes, swallows, herons.

This was where Ersilia's mother would have washed the family's clothes, where the little girl would have bathed with her older sister in the cool shallows, and watched their brother catch fish in his handkerchief. I imagined her picking the tiny grey flowers that moved like dancers in the breeze on the riverbanks, keeping an eye out for rats and grass snakes. After the rains, she may have collected tadpoles from puddles on the road and returned them to the river so they could grow into frogs.

The Samoggia could be temperamental and when the river flooded, as it regularly did, a watchman kept guard around the clock. His oil lamp burnt through the night, scaring away the foxes, badgers, hares and martens that came to drink after sunset. But most of the time the river's power was something to respect, not fear.

On Google Maps I located the river. I saw a bridge, a cluster of post-war shops and houses and, surrounding them, flat, cultivated fields and grey industrial pockets. The river is lined with a bank of thick vegetation made up of precarious plant populations, including poplars and willows no taller than 5 or 6 metres. The trees, I read, are rooted in gravelly, sandy soils which are often subject to inundation that sometimes breaks up and destroys the vegetation, making their existence a tenuous one.

From all this I gleaned that Ersilia's early years were tranquil, conventional, secure – not unlike mine. Ersilia's household was poor. But she was nestled in the bosom of a family where males were outnumbered by females, who would have filled the ramshackle dwelling with their chatter, cooking, darning. She likely felt safe and loved. Ersilia would have had every reason to hope that her existence by the Samoggia would continue, that she would grow up to have the kind of life her parents had.

Piecing together the series of events that began when she turned six, it was clear that a metaphorical inland tsunami was headed her way. In the space of two years, it destroyed everything good in its path, as the life she had assumed was rooted and dependable was swept away.

The string of bereavements, the letter revealed, began with the death of Ersilia's older sister in 1871. Child mortality wasn't uncommon for children of wage labourers in the rural areas of Bologna, with almost half dying before reaching fifteen (Ernesta was eight). Still, this must have come as a blow to the family. The girl died in February, winter. I thought of the family's cold house with unsealed doors and windows and a leaking roof that let in the wind. What killed her? Pneumonia, bronchitis? Maybe it had something to do with a nutritional deficiency because of their inadequate diet.

I wondered how her sister's passing changed Ersilia's relationship with her mother. Did Enrica hold her tighter? Ersilia was the eldest daughter now, with new responsibilities. She had seen her first dead body. Her beloved big sister – whom she'd looked up to, who had looked out for her – now lay beneath a mound of dirt in the ground.

Four months later, the family was hit again, this time by the death of the children's nonna. Maria Anna was seventy-three. The remaining family members got on with their lives. It was summer. Teodoro and the others would have continued with the hemp work, only now Ersilia was probably required to prepare the *minestra* ahead of their return; she had to learn to cook. Her mother was still breastfeeding one-year-old Argia, but she could no longer leave the baby with the grandmother when she went to work. Ersilia's duties were piling up.

Two years later Enrica was pregnant again. I wondered if the experienced mother knew, from the pointed shape of her belly, that her unborn child was a boy, as the Anzolesi believed, and rejoiced (the birth of a female was considered a tragedy by farming families). Or were there difficulties, warning signs in the pregnancy, which only the midwife knew about?

Here arrived the next blow, from which Ersilia's family never recovered. The family lost its matriarch. This was the critical paragraph in the letter from San Giovanni in Persiceto, the tragic turning point in Ersilia's life that explained so much:

> Enrica died on 26.5.1874, almost certainly in childbirth because on the same date the couple's last child, Serra Vincenzo, was born and died a few months later on 28.11.1874.

Enrica was thirty-six. The midwife would have been alone in the bedroom with her when it happened and then had to deliver the terrible news to Teodoro, who was likely waiting in the kitchen. The other children would have been sent away to a neighbour's house ahead of the birth and learnt about their mother's death on their return. I couldn't help but think of that night listening to Olivia Newton-John when my mother was in hospital giving birth to my baby brother. Ersilia was also eight. Vincenzo was named for Enrica's father (her mother was Cristina).

Teodoro was thirty-nine, halfway through his life – he would live to eighty. Bereft. It was not uncommon, at that time and place, for a man to lose his spouse while still caring for dependent children. More men than women remarried after becoming widowed, but as a penniless labourer with four children ranging from newborn to thirteen, Teodoro would not have made a desirable husband. Critically, for Ersilia's life's course, he did not remarry.

As the eldest surviving female, Ersilia found herself being forced to assume the wifely responsibilities of her mother. In a society where women performed all domestic duties, this young girl would have had to do all the cooking, washing and cleaning for the household, as well as care for her newborn brother and infant sister. I imagined her shock, confusion, her bottled-up grief. Her mother was gone; she was the only mother now. Losing Enrica at such an age forced Ersilia into a liminal state, neither child nor adult.

Ersilia's losses didn't stop there, however. Baby Vincenzo, deprived of a mother's milk, died at six months. A year after Enrica's death, the diminished family of four moved to an isolated house, not part of a hamlet or any residential settlement, in Zenerigolo, a parish in the Persicetan countryside. There they remained for three years, after which time they relocated to the urban centre of San Giovanni. When they arrived, there were only three of them. Shortly before Teodoro removed his family from the countryside for good, he sent the youngest child, Argia, away. She was six years old and would never return to her family. Possibly she went to live with relatives, or else became a domestic servant in a wealthy household. Such things were common in settings of rural poverty, especially in northern Italy.

Argia's banishment was the final childhood loss for Ersilia, the last female remaining with an older brother and a father to look after. She'd lost her older sister, grandmother, mother, baby brother and now the younger sister she'd reared for three years. Losing Argia would have been gut-wrenching; Ersilia's sense of helplessness must have felt profound, like drowning. Learning this, I wondered if having her sister taken from her prepared her for what she would have to do with Natalina. Did it form an emotional callus? Did it make abandoning her daughter easier because she'd already lost a sister she'd treated like a daughter?

By the time Teodoro moved his remaining family members to their squalid accommodation in San Giovanni on Via Donzelle – the same street where midwife Rosa Rizzi resided – Ersilia was almost thirteen and working as a domestic servant to support her father, who was likely unemployed. Her brother was almost eighteen and a hemp worker. Enrico would have travelled each day into the nearby countryside looking for work, returning to the city at night. The family moved again four more times, always remaining in the tight centre of San Giovanni. Their penultimate address was on Via Umberto (many of the streets have since been renamed), where Paolino was born in 1891. Finally, the family moved to Via Abate in 1897, where Natalina entered the world a year later.

The discovery that an older brother lived with Ersilia and her father introduced a new layer of murkiness into her situation, a new potential source of threat and vulnerability. Enrico didn't marry until forty, uncommonly late for a male at the time; only 5 per cent of men wed for the first time at this age or after. I didn't know what to make of this information. Should I have felt anxious for Ersilia? Was it Enrico who paid the fee to the Bastardini hospital, so that she wouldn't have to be locked up in the foundling home and wet-nurse other babies? Was

Enrico, not Teodoro, the monster? Did Ersilia want to protect Natalina from him? Was there any point in speculating about something that was so utterly unknowable?

I would never know the paternity of Ersilia's children. The bare facts were these. Ersilia's household, from before the onset of her teenage years, comprised herself and two older males to whom she was enslaved domestically. There was no woman to guide her through puberty, no-one to turn to when she got her first period, to teach her about sex and pregnancy. Ersilia's life wasn't hers to direct, not in any meaningful way. Whether bound by a sense of duty, or something else, Ersilia remained shackled to her father. There would be no opportunity to marry, no chance of a conventional family life.

The findings about Ersilia's early life spurred me on to search for details about Argia. What became of her, after her father sent her away?

Ersilia's little sister, I discovered, returned to San Giacomo as an adult when she went to live with her fiancé, a shoemaker she married four months later, aged twenty-three. By then Argia had a profession: she was a seamstress. The couple's daughter was born in San Giovanni in Persiceto the following year. Argia and the shoemaker married one month before the birth, meaning she would have been heavily pregnant at the time (pregnant brides in Bologna's agricultural periphery were commonplace). Argia had five legitimate children, two boys and three girls, just like her mother.

What I learnt about Argia helped me to see the bigger narrative of Ersilia's life – namely, what a cataclysmic event the death of her mother was for her as the eldest remaining female of her family. I realised how lucky Argia was that her father offloaded her, as it liberated her from the burdens Ersilia had to carry. It was clear that nobody in Teodoro's household felt the death of his wife as much as Ersilia, that nobody paid for the family's tragedy as she did in the loss of opportunity, security and happiness.

This was how I answered that question, posed when I first took on my great-grandmother's story, of how to make sense of her abandonment. There was a convergence here of social narrative and lived experience. It was the combination of a coercive religious moral code that constrained Ersilia's choices around her pregnancies, along with the family dramas uncovered in the municipal archives and revealed in that letter, that conspired to condemn her to a future where she abandoned her child. I now had some of the context of Ersilia's act. I didn't know whether ultimately it was the family's poverty or something more sinister that caused her to give up Natalina. But I was certain that what befell her – her powerlessness, vulnerability and impossible choices – all began with the untimely death of her own mother.

Travelling to San Giovanni the first time, a forty-minute drive from Bologna and the place where Ersilia moved to with her father and brother as a teenager, I carried a heaviness about my family's story that I was still trying to process. Milena had made an appointment for me with Dr Chiara Reatti, the young archivist from the San Giovanni Battista parish who had found Ersilia's name in 'The Book of Secret Baptisms'. She was waiting for us outside the church and took us through the back of the building, up a lift and into a meeting room. There we were greeted by the group of older women volunteers who were the source of that illuminating letter about Ersilia's childhood.

The five women were carefully dressed in neck scarves and brooches. They had brought along folders of papers as well as various historical baptism books – both the official volumes, dating back to 1566, and the secret ones. The women, it became evident, were self-appointed custodians of their town's hidden history of unwed mothers and abandoned children. It was their work, when a curious descendant came searching for a mother, to rouse that history from where it lay slumbering in the archives, to stir up the silence that surrounded the woman's experiences, allowing her truth to be told. The women interlaced that history with an affection for their town and its traditions, which they were eager to share with us that day. We were moved by their sincerity as they shared with us old photographs of the labourers at the hemp plantations and explained how the process of extracting the fibres and producing the textiles worked.

Our meeting concluded with one of the women slicing up a chocolate cake she had made. The volunteers then produced their most generous surprise of all: two beautiful pieces of handcrafted hemp cloth which, one of the women explained, trilling her r's like a bird, were called *chiaretto*. They were the size of small towels, used for drying glasses, and they were gifts for us. Creamy-coloured, they had two kinds of weave – one tighter, one looser – with a fringe at each end and tiny loose threads and kinks that made the pieces unique. The hemp smelt clean and earthy and was as pretty as lace, though coarser and less dainty. Rubbing the soft fringe between my fingers, it struck me that this was my knotty heritage.

Dr Reatti had offered to show us the house where Natalina was born, so we left the women and crossed the recently resurfaced central square, Piazza del Popolo. It was paved in concentric circles in homage to the original design of the medieval town, which was also known as Borgo Rotondo, 'round village'. The church, with its neoclassical façade and adjacent 800-year-old clocktower, dominated the piazza. On a subsequent trip to San Giovanni, I would learn about a minor church scandal that took place the year of Natalina's birth. It involved a nineteenth-century painting by two Bolognese brothers, Alberto and Fabio Fabbi, of the town's patron saint, St John the Baptist. Their depiction of Herod's daughter was considered to be so 'sexy', with her painted face and jewellery, that the priest removed the painting from the altar (it was subsequently returned).

I counted a dozen people in the square; this town was not on tourist maps. Ersilia's house was two blocks from the church.

The sky had clouded over by the time we stood outside Ersilia's building on narrow Via Abate, the place where she lived almost forty years until moving to Bologna in 1935. Boarded up and decayed, it was the most neglected property on a street populated by herbalists and wellness shops. Four small windows on the upper floors were covered over with faded grey timber boards. A brown roller shutter hid what I assumed was the old shop window. The patchy façade was mossy green under the eaves and windowsills. Elsewhere the tan render had peeled away, like flaking skin after a bad sunburn, exposing large sections of red bricks and wiring.

A bank of lush weeds spilled out from behind a tall metal fence that reached across the entire building frontage. The edifice pressed up against the road with nowhere to shelter from the weather. There was no footpath, balcony, portico, awning – no architectural embellishment apart from a rusty air vent over the chained front door. External lanterns had been stripped away, leaving behind metal fixtures which hung like four lost quavers plucked from a music score. The building was so bare it looked two-dimensional, like the flat backdrop to a stage set. The apartment, I knew from studying Google Maps, had no shared external courtyard to speak of: nowhere to hang washing, nowhere to plant herbs. Being poor, Ersilia's family would have inhabited the top floor, with its oppressive, sloped ceiling.

Viewing the building in person that day, I felt an array of emotions.

Disbelief that we were there, occupying the same ground she once did. Looking at the same scene she saw every day, returning from work or lugging home heavy buckets of water from the public fountain.

Gratitude that the building still existed so I could witness its materiality. Ersilia may have believed she left no evidence of herself with her daughter by not placing a broken medallion inside her swaddling. Yet here was her dilapidated house, still standing where it had for hundreds of years. Walls that would have absorbed her bodily and cooking smells. Walls that might still bear her marks: an oily stain of black soot from the fires she lit every other day; a perforation where she'd pinned a picture of the Madonna.

I also felt compassion. Inside that wretched apartment, on a wintry December morning 120 years ago, Ersilia gave birth in a damp and mouldy room to a daughter she cared enough about to have in the presence of a midwife.

Standing there in front of the house, I pictured the copper cauldron with boiled water. The bed covered by protective straw or corncob leaves. The midwife's instruments – stethoscope, thermometer, rubber probe, forceps, acids, soap, cotton, scissors – laid out on the table. The lump of roasted chestnuts to nourish the baby on its long journey.

And I saw Ersilia in a way I hadn't before: the woman the midwife left behind. Her aching body leaking like an unseaworthy vessel. Milk oozing from her engorged breasts, bloody secretions congealing in her undergarments, stubborn tears pooling in the corners of her eyes. I imagined the thoughts that must have passed through her mind as she burned the stained strips of hemp cloth and soiled straw used to mop the blood and protect the bedding from the mess of the labour. How she might have wished that, like a boat in peril, she could have succumbed to eternal rest on the seabed. And I wondered what it was like for her, the moment she said goodbye to her baby daughter, because she thought someone else – anyone else – could do a better job of looking after her than she could.

Rainer Maria Rilke wrote in 'The Second Elegy' that:

> . . . the houses
> that we live in still stand. We alone
> fly past all things, as fugitive as the wind.
> And all things conspire to keep silent about us, half
> out of shame perhaps, half as unutterable hope.

Ersilia's life had flown past 'as fugitive as the wind'. Yet her abandonment of Natalina was a seismic event in our family's history, the rupture that happens when two blocks of the earth suddenly slip past each other. Her act changed the course of all our lives. Whatever shame and other torments befell her happened because she was poor, unlucky, and a woman. Her suffering had been wiped from the official record, rendered invisible, silent, like it had never happened. But here in San Giovanni, a group of curious and sympathetic women had come together to prevent her story being obliterated from history. Her 'unutterable hope' that she would one day be understood, finally realised.

My mother spent several nights at the Crown Street Women's Hospital with our baby brother, who was badly jaundiced. Our father picked them up from the hospital.

I don't remember the moment they returned home. Was I waiting excitedly by the front door for my mother? Did my heart leap as I saw her walk through our green metal front gate carrying the newest member of our family?

Either way, I know it came as a relief to have my mother back with us, to know that life could now return to normal. My anxiety about her abandonment of us was allayed.

7
Forgiveness

Natalina's life plays in my mind like one of those old-fashioned animation flipbooks but backwards. It begins with the images my mother furnished of her Nonna Lina, who died when she was eight. A kindly nonna stuffing lollies, fruit and nuts into stockings for the grandchildren on the *La Befana* (Epiphany) feast day. A celebrated cook shaping potato gnocchi into pillows for her daughters' dinner. A devoted wife shining the shoes of the husband she worshipped, my mother says, 'like a slave'.

Next comes my discovery of her abandonment. Back, back I go. I get lost in the pages I uncover in the archives detailing her life as a foundling, becoming preoccupied by her motherless childhood. I read that she was raised from the age of two by millers from the Apennine Mountains. I ask my mother but she is perplexed, knowing nothing about any foster parents. We search the family papers for correspondence, find a postcard Natalina's youngest daughter sent her father after her mother's death. On the front are images of Bologna landmarks. On the back is written: *La città di mamma.* It's all my mother knows of Natalina's early life: that she had no parents and came from Bologna.

In trying to imagine her childhood, I was reaching for a lost memory. History, it is said, is written from what sources can be salvaged; once

I'd exhausted these, I had inference, what could be intuited in the gaps. Words, with their unsettled meanings, were the mortar between my bricks as I reimagined a formless past. I never asked my nonna about her mother, so will never know what Natalina told her daughters about her childhood – whether she told them anything. All I could go on was my mother's knowledge of her Nonna Lina, which is limited to those meagre facts that were relayed to her and from which I inferred (rightly or wrongly) no people existed in Natalina's shared memories, only places.

Then I learnt she was a sickly child who suffered, among other maladies: malnutrition, scrofula (a tuberculosis infection of the lymph nodes), abscesses and lesions, all within her first four years under the millers' care. When the Bologna archivists told me there was likely a connection between the illnesses she suffered and the type of work her foster parents did, I knew I had found an answer to the question of why Natalina never spoke about them as an adult: she was a child-slave, probably forced to carry sacks of flour from a tender age.

Vincenzo Bigondi and Liduina Venusta Calzolari were both twenty-nine when they collected their infant foundling from the Bastardini hospital. Typically, the miller was a central figure in rural society: respected because he knew how to harness the flow of the river to transform those precious grains of wheat into flour; envied because he was often wealthier than other peasants. The couple undoubtedly wished for a son to help in their milling business and would have been disappointed not to have one.

Foundlings were the ultimate form of cheap labour among the lower classes, requiring minimal food and no pay. In exchange for feeding and keeping her clean, for committing to educating her morally, religiously and civilly, her foster parents were supplied with clothing, medical care and a monthly wage which decreased as Natalina aged and her value as a worker grew.

For their first five years together, the foster family lived in Vincenzo's birthplace in Loiano, 35 kilometres south of Bologna, in the village of Querceto, named for the nearby towering forest of oaks, on Via di Molino della Pozza, 'mill of the puddle'. Being Vincenzo's village, many of his relatives would have lived there too. That Natalina never took his name – she always remained Mirci – provides an insight into how the millers regarded her. And how she regarded them.

I spent a morning with my researcher, Milena, at the Archivio di Stato di Bologna, searching for the 'mill of the puddle' in its collection of nineteenth-century maps. In a room with arched timber windows overlooking a courtyard and a large oak tree, the archivists helped us unearth a series of maps from 1885 labelled 'Querceto'. From them we concluded the miller's village was located by a small river, which stood to reason, given the mill's reliance on hydropower.

I imagined a stone house set on the bank of a fast-running river, surrounded by rock walls, grazing animals, pear trees. And that mill: a mechanical beast that would have frightened a young child with its insatiable hunger. I saw the water gushing and splashing and turning the waterwheel over, felt the rumbling of the millstones grinding the grain that Vincenzo would have poured in from above the chute. It would have been Natalina's job to collect the crushed wheat in bags at the bottom, trying hard not to spill the precious flour, to hold up the sacks too big for her to manage alone. All the while, white powder would have covered her body, hair and clothes, becoming lodged in her eyebrows and eyelashes, under her fingernails, in the crevices in her skin. Making her cough.

Eventually it must have become too much because when she turned fourteen, she appeared at the front door of the Bastardini hospital and begged them to take her in. The family was living in Bologna by then, on Via San Petronio Vecchio behind the Santo Stefano complex. I pictured her distress, what her foster parents might have done to provoke her into taking such a drastic step. Was it the nature of the work they forced her to do, or how much? Did they heap insults upon her and beat her? The words were scrawled in red at the bottom of her page in the wet-nurse register: 'Claimed maltreatment – left for now at the Esposta.' (*Esposta*, 'exposed', was another name for Bologna's foundling home). It was a brave act on Natalina's part: wilful and independent. Such claims were taken seriously by the Bastardini; as the guardian of female foundlings' honour, the hospital would have taken her away from her foster parents if she was suffering abuse. Ultimately, though, the institution regarded the situation as not serious enough to warrant her permanent removal, so Natalina returned to the millers.

Was it any wonder she regarded her life in foster care as best forgotten, as my mother's complete lack of knowledge of this part of her life suggests she did? Perhaps it was easier to pretend she didn't have a life before her marriage because she didn't want to burden her loved ones with her past. I imagined the hurt and shame she must have endured. The stigma of illegitimacy would have weighed heavily; until a law change in 1955, a child's illegitimate status had to be recorded on all their official papers. When did she discover she was a foundling, and how did the knowledge arrive? I pondered Natalina's feelings towards the woman who consigned her to such a life. How did it feel, knowing her mother didn't want her? I recalled that ripped birth record, with the missing word *mamma*, my initial assumption that she tore it in a fit of rage. Did she struggle with forgiveness over her lifetime?

After the plane crash I had a falling out with a close friend that lasted a decade.

We had been a significant part of each other's lives since we were twelve. We had always been there for each other in difficult times, and my friend quite reasonably wanted to be there for me now. Unknown to me, she had re-organised her life to support me through my recovery, including weaning her baby daughter early.

I could not, however, bear to have longstanding friends – people who knew the old me – around. Not in those first weeks and months in Perth, where I was hospitalised. I was already dealing with my own grief and that of my family and to take on any more felt unendurable. Understandably, my friend was frustrated and wounded by my refusal to let her perform the role she so ardently wanted to.

We spoke on the phone, and I promised that as soon as I returned home, she could visit me.

Six months later I returned with Michael to Canberra to continue my rehabilitation. It was a gruelling regime, five full days a week at the hospital, followed by hours of scar tissue massage at home. By Friday night, I was beyond exhausted.

On the weekend that my friend's visit was to take place, I couldn't get out of bed. I phoned her to say we would have to postpone. Having waited for this moment for so long, my friend was distressed. She later called me back and poured out her hurt. 'If I can't see you, I can't help you,' she said.

We didn't speak for a long time after that. My friend tried many times to contact me, but I could not get past what I perceived she had done: put her own suffering ahead of mine, when I was the one who had lost my legs.

A decade later, after we moved back to Sydney, my friend and I arranged to have dinner. We went to a French restaurant down the road from my new house and talked honestly, openly, about what had transpired, what had been going on for each of us at the time. We cried and cried, the two of us sitting at a table in the window until closing. The words that cut me the most were when she told me that I had missed watching her children grow up.

I fear too much time has passed, that we will never get the chance to rebuild our friendship back to where it was. The knowledge of this – of those lost ten years – pains me deeply. If only she had allowed me more time. If only I had been able to forgive her sooner.

I think it is unfortunate that, as children raised in the Catholic Church, the first lesson you learn about forgiveness comes around the age of seven when you are compelled, before taking First Holy Communion, to undergo the frightening ordeal of confessing, one on one, to a priest.

I remember the confession box of my primary school years. A daunting wooden stall at the side of the church, it was divided into three components. The priest sat in the middle, his face obscured behind a lattice grate, while the young penitents lined up one on either side, waiting for their turn. The days beforehand were spent trying to think of the worst that we, small children who barely knew how to tie our shoelaces, had done in our few short years on earth. I wrestle with the knowledge that in sending my son to a Catholic school, I forced him to undergo the same ritual that I found so senseless.

The message this rite teaches children is that, first and foremost, they are sinners. It is a lesson in self-loathing that never leaves you – when what really matters is that children understand that to be human is to make mistakes. And that holding onto bitterness for perceived transgressions against us can stifle growth and life and lead to awful regret.

Today, I struggle with the concept of forgiveness. I know forgiving is hard work, that it can take a lifetime, and may not come even then. I know that sometimes the most we can strive for, when someone has wronged us gravely, is humility: to be able to accept that none of us is perfect. I struggle to forgive the pilot who crashed the plane and took my legs, who sentenced me to a life where I can never be the mother I would have been if not for his actions. I try to remember the treatment of the adulterous woman, when Jesus, calling out hypocrisy, told the Pharisees, 'Whichever one of you has committed no sin may throw the first stone.'

Michael steered our rental car southwest through the Reno Valley, along a winding road with hairpin turns. There were no footpaths, just long stretches of retaining walls propping up small hamlets interspersed with cultivated fields and pockets of untamed vegetation, and road signs warning of bounding deer. Milena was with us. We were headed to Gaggio Montano, a small community in the Apennines, close to the Tuscan border.

We were following the trail left by another Bologna foundling, a mayor of the mountains who spent his whole life searching for his mother. Giorgio Sirgi once sent her a remarkable message through an Italian journalist. It was after the initial release of his book, *I Bastardini*, a collection of testimonies from abandoned children. Its publication in 1994 coincided with the period when the foundling home's work was coming to an end. It is unlikely she received it:

> I wanted to know not only who she was and who I was. If she had abandoned me out of misery or dishonour, I had now become a young adult, able to take charge of her, no hard feelings. If she was in need, I just wanted to say: Mum, I'm here.

Sirgi died without finding his mother. I knew I could learn something from this man's legacy. A foundling abandoned not once but twice – the second time by foster parents he had believed were his own – yet who harboured no rancour.

Up, up we climbed. In the distance we watched the rugged mountain chain unfold. Peaks covered by woodland: fir, beech and oak trees. And below them, vast expanses of quiet, grassy valleys, the population dispersed into clusters of small villages. Then closer in, by the roadside, a lone rickety timber shed, scattered rustic stone cottages, shuttered villas, the odd church steeple. The people largely invisible, apart from their different-coloured skip bins.

Sirgi's story was typical. Born in Bologna in 1928 to a mother who 'didn't want to be named', he was farmed out to a wet nurse who returned him to the foundling home once he was weaned. At age three, he was given to foster parents who already had two birth daughters.

When the foster parents welcomed a biological son, they returned the foundling to the Bastardini. To calm him down – for the six-year-old's instincts told him something terrible was happening – his foster mother let him hold her purse. When the paperwork was signed, she asked for her purse back, telling the boy she was going to buy a bag of lollies. He never saw her again. The disillusionment and pain of that second abandonment marked his life.

As I grappled with my great-grandmother's abandonment, Sirgi's story and those documented in his book brought to life the foundling's existence. That moment of disbelief when the little boy or girl first realised their mother had given them away. Sometimes, if they'd only lived in an institution, they learnt this from older foundlings returned by foster parents. Then, as young adults, the new agony when those lucky few, against all odds, found their mother, only to have her reject them all over again out of fear their secret shame would be exposed.

Sirgi spoke of how the foundling's need to find their mother would accompany them throughout their life, that 'it is stronger than you'. This was echoed by the Bologna archivists, who told me two kinds of foundlings came searching: those who believed they were the children of famous or noble people and sought an inheritance; and those of a certain age who possessed a powerful urge to understand where they came from. Dr Bongiovanni called these latter foundlings the 'more desperate projects'.

> They know they were brought up by an adoptive family but don't know who their parents are, and in front of them they don't see anything other than the end of their lives. Maybe over the course of their life they haven't paid much attention to this but as they get older, and closer to an age that brings greater reflection, they have a sense of urgency to know these roots, to at least know a name.

The archivists can't help these foundlings because of the law preventing them revealing the mother's name for 100 years. They knew of only one case where a foundling was able to discover her mother's identity in the archives. She turned up on her 100th birthday; she had waited a century, just for a name.

Through his compassion for the mothers, Sirgi showed me another way to think about women like Ersilia. For all the foundlings' pain, it was the mothers to whom he dedicated his book. He implored readers not to despise the single mothers forced by fate to forsake their 'babies in swaddling'. He never judged these women who were looked down upon by society as having low morals, who often found themselves in impossible situations, confronted with excruciating choices. But nor did he judge his fellow foundlings – whom he regarded as siblings – when they couldn't forgive their mothers.

A preface to Sirgi's book points out that, above all, the women's abandonment of their children was the result of social, moral, cultural and material conditions of 'unimaginable marginalisation and exploitation'. Conditions that included men who refused responsibility, poor families living in 'ignorance and backwardness', rich families living in 'hypocrisy and self-righteousness', and the absence of contraception or sex education.

In the area of the Bolognese Apennines until the early 1950s, especially in the agricultural sector, families were ruled by the patriarch. Young men enjoyed a freedom that was a prerogative of their sex while the women were virtual slaves of their families, and the subject of malicious talk by neighbours. Whatever circumstances led to an illegitimate pregnancy, the fault always lay with the woman. Punished, beaten, name-called, scorned, humiliated, she was forced to hide away to spare her family the shame of a visible pregnancy for as long as possible. Until, 'slowly slowly', solutions would emerge. Leave the baby on the steps of a church; commit infanticide – painful but resolute, even if it risked jail; give birth in an institute then abandon the newborn; give birth at home and leave the baby with the midwife. The testimonies made clear that, from the moment of abandonment, the mother's life would never be the same, that the only way of not going mad was to put up a psychological defence and act as though it never happened.

Included in Sirgi's book was one mother's account. At age fifteen, the woman worked as a domestic for a wealthy family far from home. She formed a relationship with one of the family's sons and fell pregnant to him. The family forbade them from marrying, intercepted the pregnant girl's letters to her parents seeking help, and sent her to Bologna where she was taken to a midwife's house. When her baby was born, the family arranged for him to be dispatched to the Bastardini hospital. After she returned home, the girl tried but was never allowed to see her son. Thirty years on, he found her. By now married with legitimate children, the woman suggested to her husband that they invite her son to meet their family. The husband refused and begged her to never see him again. The woman, afraid that if her legitimate children knew her secret it would compromise their love for her, apologised to her abandoned son and told him she could not see him anymore. Then she buried the terrible hurt, believing her suffering was penance for what she did at fifteen.

I asked my mother to help translate the testimony and afterwards she rang me to read out Sirgi's final passage: 'I hope that this story will be read by numerous people who still have their mother so that they can ask, "Mum, this isn't you, is it?"' My mother wanted to know if she had understood the author's meaning correctly. I told her yes, I thought so. He wanted every person with a mother to ask her whether she had a secret child. This was so that they might then reassure her that if she did, they would love her just the same. All he knew was his own experience, that of being a foundling. And in his mind, any mother could be his.

Previously, I'd thought of unconditional love as something enlightened parents offered their children, but Sirgi's appeal to children to love their mothers this way turned the notion on its head. What do we mean by unconditional love?

For me it means total acceptance. A love that endures disappointments and hurts; a love that forgives. A love that comes back. A love without end.

I do not doubt my parents' love for me. Sometimes, however, parental love doesn't always feel unconditional, even if – when tested – it ultimately proves to be. Parents' love is bound up in wanting what is 'best' for their child. As such, they tend to impose on offspring their own ideas of how they should be and what constitutes a good life. Hopes may be measured against the achievements and disappointments parents have experienced in their own lives, and can become entangled in their expectations for their children. The message this sends, perhaps unjustly, is one of conditionality. It can also breed an unhealthy, lifelong need for others' approval. As a parent, it can be hard to let go of these projections one has for one's children. I know, for I grapple with this myself.

My relationship with my parents casts a shadow over my own parenting. There were certain ways I was parented – loudly, over-protectively, being pushed to achieve – that I promised I would not repeat with my own child. As a newly minted mother, I swore to myself that my child would not grow up thinking that to be loved, he needed to please me. Then, wanting to give him opportunities I never had, I enrolled him in violin and piano lessons and pushed him to continue even when he told me he didn't enjoy them. When he didn't want to join the debating team, I tried to guilt him into doing it, having been a champion debater in high school who saw the value it offered me in my career as a lawyer (work I later abandoned for journalism). He would be letting his teachers down, I told him, if he didn't. It is excruciating writing this; I was wrong to do it.

Over the years I have frequently checked in to see if I've kept that promise to my newborn. I find myself looking over my shoulder in case my parents are there, in the umbra. I contemplate the high school grievances I still hold against them. The public upbraiding by the front gate the one time I ever flunked a maths test. Though I would never do that to my son, I wonder: am I so different? The truth is that the things I so resented being pressed upon me are the same things I want for my child – that any parent does: to keep him safe; for him to make the most of the opportunities that are available; for him to have a fulfilling life.

Our Volvo followed Gaggio Montano's curved, tree-lined main street, neat with paved footpaths, benches and plain shuttered buildings of muted shades of apricot and tan, until we arrived at Arnaldo Brasa Piazza. We saw a tiered concrete fountain at the rear with nested basins. Stairs either side of the fountain connected to a landing outside the stone municipal building. At the library inside, we had arranged to meet a group of people whose lives were touched by Sirgi.

The library was basic, with walls of floor-to-ceiling metal shelves in the main section and a small partitioned-off area for children. Light entered through glass doors overlooking the piazza. In the centre of the room three square tables had been pushed together. Standing around them was a small group of people.

Mauro Brunetti, stout with a closely contoured salt-and-pepper beard, was the mayor of the neighbouring municipality of Castel di Casio. He described Sirgi as a father figure. Adelfo Cecchelli and his wife, Margarete Bunje, ran *Gente di Gaggio*, 'People of Gaggio', the local cultural association that helped finance Sirgi's book, republished after his death. Giuseppe Mingarelli was a foundling. His connection to Sirgi went back to when he was a boy, and the mayor rescued him from a Turin foundling home.

Giuseppe was neatly attired in a button-up navy vest and khaki shirt and had bright blue eyes. Born in 1954, he told us he was abandoned anonymously as a baby by his mother in a *pozzo*, a well or an underground depression. He explained that in the foundling home where he lived there were two classes of children: those who had families that could not provide for them but visited at Christmas and Easter, and those who didn't have families. The latter group had to inform the other children when their families had come to see them.

'We'd go to these kids and tell them, "Look, your mum and dad have arrived." And we would accompany them to the visit. It was a very difficult role for us.'

Giuseppe's manner was so artless, so matter-of-fact, it was as though we were hearing not the sixty-four-year-old man, but the suffering child that still lay within. Giuseppe said that while walking a child to their parents, he would request they ask them for an extra lolly for him, because he had no-one to ask. Afterwards he would question himself why he didn't have parents.

'You don't know the answer. You torment yourself.'

My researcher's voice cracked translating the word *caramela*, 'lolly'. Perhaps it was because a lolly represented a child's innocence; it was also meagre, a wholly inadequate substitute for a parent's affections. I felt consoled by Milena's tears, knowing I was not the only one who felt weighed down by the foundling story, unravelled by it. I wanted to hug my son, reassure him how loved he was. It was unbearable to think of any child feeling as alone in the world as Giuseppe had felt.

As a foundling who spent years moving between different institutions, Giuseppe told us he continued to hope a family would adopt him. Sirgi was mayor in 1967 when a childless farming couple from Castel di Casio approached him asking for a favour. They were looking for a child to adopt, a foundling like himself. The search to fulfil their request led Sirgi to Turin.

The couple was disappointed upon discovering that the boy who looked six (from malnutrition) was in fact twelve, too old for anyone to want to adopt. The boy, Giuseppe, begged them to try him out, assuring them if they didn't like him, they could always send him back. The couple offered to take him for a summer holiday. Giuseppe said of course he would go, but they needed to know he was looking for a mother and father forever, like all children. There was silence until the couple replied they wanted a son forever too. Giuseppe said from that moment his adoptive parents treated him like a natural son, and he eventually took their name.

Sirgi's extraordinary compassion for the mothers of foundlings was not shared by all his fraternity of abandoned children, as Giuseppe made clear. He told us that when his mother asked to see him, many years after his adoption, he refused to meet her. He didn't want to disappoint his adoptive parents, who had shown him a good life.

'Whereas she, sometime just after I was born, stuck me in a well. You can't come looking for me when I'm older.'

By then Giuseppe knew he was one of six biological children born to different fathers, and his mother was a prostitute. The first time he saw his mother, she was lying in a casket at her funeral.

'I had never seen her, and how often I had looked for her.'

Giuseppe's struggle to accept his mother's actions was a reminder that sometimes mothers do unsettling things that can be difficult to reconcile, no matter the extenuating circumstances. I grappled with comprehending how, as with the mother in Sirgi's book, a woman's fear of being discovered could be stronger than her desire to be reunited with her abandoned child. Or that one kind of love – for legitimate children – could be stronger than the love for an illegitimate child. Or if not that, then how the desire for conformity and social acceptance could trump maternal love of any kind.

But then, perhaps it was my own need for conventionality that caused me to feel troubled by some of these women's mothering in the first place.

One of my dear friends, a single woman with a successful career, decided to have children alone. I was encouraging and supportive of her decision, giving her the lucky charm that had, I half believed, helped me to conceive my own child.

We were having breakfast at a café one day, discussing her plans to place her baby into childcare so she could return to work. She expressed her reservations over having to do this, at which point I all too eagerly agreed that childcare centres were dreadful places for babies. I was blindsided when my friend took umbrage and couldn't, for a long time, understand why she had. She knew that I too had applied to put my own son into the university's childcare facility, so Michael could return to work while I pursued academia.

Reflecting on her reaction later, I saw how traditional my views on raising young children were. They had been shaped by my upbringing, where my mother only returned to work after her last child started school. This belief still held sway, even though I had witnessed her frustrations and disappointments over having been denied a career because of the demands of family (first her parents, then her husband and children).

When Michael decided to delay going back to work, I was spared from having to make a choice that was difficult for me because I only knew one way of 'mothering' (even if, in my situation, the stay-at-home parent was the father). My friend had wanted reassurance, and I gave her my judgement.

We were on Via del Pratello in Bologna, gazing up at a two-storey, terracotta-coloured house with a timber, arch-framed door. Upstairs, where the window shutters were thrown open, whimsical pots of yellow flowers and pink succulents spilled over a ledge like sunbursts. The millers moved here when Natalina was seven. It was the first of many moves, geographic mobility being typical of workers in the early 1900s when the spreading city became an increasingly powerful magnet.

The name Pratello referenced a distant era, when the street lay outside the city's walls and was a country lane in a grassy, uncultivated area awash with waterways and mills (*prato* means 'meadow'). Evidence of its more bucolic past could still be found nearby: a fragment of the Reno Canal here, a bronze statue of a naked washerwoman there, commemorating those who once worked the same canal. Via del Pratello straddled urban and country life, and the millers were following the canals.

Today Via del Pratello is the city's bohemian district and a favourite of students. Lined with bars, taverns, theatre companies and craft workshops, these establishments recall the protests of the 1960s and '70s when the street hosted political movements. Windows are barred and at noon, when we visited, shutters were lowered like a sleepy hipster's drooping eyelids. The porticoes were plainer here, the buildings grungier and less ornamental, though brightened by graffiti and street art. A blue roller door featuring a half-woman, half-lion figure, with red claws and *girl power* written across a hind leg, caught my eye.

Back in 1906, this street of shifting identities was a degraded place of poverty and desperation populated by the underclass; a hangout for pimps and thieves. There would have been nothing of the meadow about it: littered with rat-infested piles of rubbish, smelling like an open sewer, and noisy after dark with leering drunks and *donne di strada*, 'women of the street'. The family didn't stay there long.

But this period in Natalina's childhood intrigued me. Her notes in the wet-nurse register suggested a change in circumstances that was not spelt out, and that the archivists could not explain. From this point, her life became disrupted as she was sent away from the millers for extended periods. A pattern commenced of frequent hospitalisations and respite trips to the seaside. She was hospitalised for a fortnight in 1907, a month in 1909, two months in 1911. Most intriguingly, she was sent to the seaside twice, for six weeks in mid-1907, and the following summer for another three.

The pertinent entries in the wet-nurse register read: 'at the sea baths', 'sent to the sea baths'. Further digging revealed these trips were arranged by the foundling home's medical inspectors. They were overseen by a charity known as l'Opera Pia degli Ospizi Marini (the Marine Hospice Charity) for children suffering from scrofula in Bologna. Scrofulous foundlings between the ages of four and twelve were sent to coastal towns on the Adriatic to be looked after by town doctors and the charity's health officials: boys to Riccione in Emilia-Romagna and girls to Fano, further south in the Marche region.

The foundling home records showed Natalina was being treated in Fano for a condition known as *linfatismo*, 'lymphatism', characterised by low vitality and swelling of the lymphatic tissue. I imagined the foundling home's doctor at work: observing the child's thin limbs and undersized stature, pressing the lumps on her neck and groin, conferring with the other foundling home staff. Then prescribing sea air, iodine salt baths, wholesome food and sunshine.

Seaside visits were unusual, the archivists told me. (I felt bizarrely proud of Natalina, hearing this, as though she must have been special to have been singled out for such rare treatment.) Natalina was also 'lucky', they said, in having just two families – first the wet nurse then the millers – when many foundlings had multiple.

Pondering the coincidence of these two pieces of good fortune, I had an inkling that they were connected, that her illnesses may have formed only part of the reason she was repeatedly sent away. The foundling home sought stability for children and offered inducements to foster parents to keep their charges. Did the mysterious seaside visits play a role in maintaining the arrangement with the millers? I developed a theory that the Bastardini, in taking her off the millers' hands for a while, prevented them returning her permanently, when – being older now and female – having to find another family for Natalina would have been difficult for the foundling home. But why would the millers have wanted respite?

Reflecting on her absences from the millers, I questioned when she first knew she was not her foster parents' biological child. Was it when the family moved to Via del Pratello, or before? Did the knowledge unfold gradually, or arrive like a blow? I thought of Sirgi, whose foster family returned him to the foundling home once their own son was born. Did the millers have a biological child?

A hunch told me something happened just before the family moved to Bologna, and that this was linked to Natalina's absences. Uncovering this could be the key to understanding how Vincenzo and Venusta (as she was known) regarded the child, whether as a daughter or a mere servant.

I wrote to the different municipalities where the family had lived, asking if any other children were recorded as living at the foster parents' addresses. Loiano, their first location, replied that their archives did not date back that far, so they could not help me.

By 1908, the millers had moved to Casalecchio di Reno, a town and municipality on the agricultural periphery of Bologna. It is where the 37-kilometre-long Reno Canal, used to transport goods in and out of the city and the location of several mills, begins. Casalecchio's demographic services were more helpful with my inquiries. An official responded to my email asking whether Natalina was the only child living at the millers' address, answering: 'Only Mrs Calzolari with her daughter and the then minor Mrs Mirci ...'

I was confused. Were the daughter and Mrs Mirci both Natalina? I applied for a 'certificate of family status' to find out.

Waiting for the certificate to arrive, I found a newspaper article about the marine hospice in Fano. There was a photograph of a large, white, three-storey building behind a wall, surrounded by trees. I read that it was built in 1885 (it has since been demolished), and operated throughout the summer season, from June to September. It could accommodate 600 people, had large, airy rooms that were used as dormitories, an 'imposing portico' and a 'pleasant loggia' that – because the hospice was built above a knoll – had panoramic views of Fano. The complex included a park 'where sporting exercises could be practised' and it was only 100 metres from the beach, 'where sea and sun therapies were administered', just beyond the railroad. I also found correspondence from 1907 between the foundling home, the marine hospice and the Bologna Chamber of Commerce, setting out the names of the dozen girls, including Natalina, receiving treatment that summer and detailing their travel arrangements.

A scene took shape in my mind: Natalina arriving on the early morning steam train from Bologna, stepping onto the platform at Fano, inhaling the tangy air, shielding her eyes from the dazzling sun.

She would have already glimpsed, from the train window, the sparkling sea that looked like a second heaven, only this one a darker blue which covered the earth. In her hand she clutched a small bundle, a piece of hemp cloth with a few possessions inside: spare socks, her bonnet, perhaps. Vice-mothers from the Fano hospice were at the station to meet all the children. They marked off the girls, each identified by a number sewn onto the fabric of their dress, and then ushered them onto the omnibus. Natalina probably wondered how long she would have to stay in Fano, why the only mother she had ever known had sent her away. Possibly she cried for Venusta that night, begged the vice-mothers to let her go home.

Over time, the salty air would have recharged her lungs, brought her a restorative calm. Having become acquainted with the other foundlings, she possibly made a friend. The girls had surnames like Ferri ('Iron'), Noci ('Walnuts'), Ambri ('Amber'), Astri ('Stars'). They ate their meals together, more eggs and fish than the girls had ever seen, at long tables in the canteen. The vice-mothers lectured them about cleanliness – each girl had her own bed, towel and handkerchief – and encouraged them to think of themselves as belonging to a large family. They must try to love each other, the women told them. The girls bathed in the sea, which was always tranquil, twice a day. None of the children would have known how to swim, so the vice-mothers may have made them hold hands and form a long line that stretched across the shore, before they walked down the beach and into the water together.

By the time the second seaside visit came around, Natalina probably wished she didn't have to return to the slums of Via del Pratello. Here by the sea, she would have enjoyed watching the sailing boats being driven along by the blustery winds, and the greedy, screeching seagulls who plunged beak first into the blue-green water. Perhaps she built up a collection of shiny pebbles that she kept hidden beneath her cot. At the marina, she may have peered into fishermen's buckets and, seeing the writhing silvery hake and grey mullet, realised what those hungry birds were catching.

The sounds of the boats jerked by the tide, creaking and clanging as they tugged at their moorings, may have comforted her, reminding her of little children pulling at the sleeves of snoozing grandfathers back in the family's village in the mountains. I imagine she didn't even mind when the wind whipped up her hair and blew sand into her eyes. She would have known, because the doctor had told her, that while the sun was turning her skin chocolate, the salty water and briny air were doing their work.

As autumn approached, Natalina likely found she was used to the rhythms of the seaside town and didn't want to leave. Or so I liked to think.

We were back in Australia when the certificate of family status arrived from Casalecchio. In disbelief I read that when Natalina's foster family arrived in the new municipality in 1908, a fourth member came with them, an infant named Maria, who bore Vincenzo's surname. I hadn't expected to be right. Natalina's foster parents had a biological daughter. This was sad news for my great-grandmother – but explained so much.

Baby Maria was born in the mountains in June 1906, just before the family moved to Via del Pratello. That year would have been a watershed for Natalina. It was probably when she learnt the truth about her origins, that the couple she believed were her natural parents were not so. The ground would have fallen away from her as awareness dawned, and she saw how her foster parents fawned over Maria, blanketing the infant with a warmth she had never felt herself.

I wondered what Venusta told Natalina. Did she tell her Maria wasn't her sister, that she, Venusta, wasn't her mother, that she and Vincenzo were paid money to look after her? Did she show her the small green instruction booklet all foster parents were given, the size of a woman's hand, and point to the section that stipulated they could send her back any time if she didn't get on and carry those heavy sacks? Did Venusta tell Natalina her actual mother didn't want her, and that was why she had given her to the Bastardini?

Poor Natalina, learning that the millers were not her real parents, that she didn't have a mother, didn't know where she came from.

People, I remind myself, are more than words. I cannot know how Natalina carried the hurt of having a mother who gave her away and withheld her identity. Whether, like Sirgi, she bore no hard feelings. Or whether, as the torn birth record suggests, she was more like Giuseppe, who, having spent his childhood searching for his mother, by adulthood did not want her to find him.

I recall that mother in Sirgi's book whose husband did not want their family to know about her abandoned son. She yielded to his wishes and suffered the loss of her boy all the years of her life, believing she deserved to be punished for what she did.

To be a mother is to carry a heavy weight. To be directly responsible for someone else – another, more vulnerable life you have brought into the world, whether you intended to or not – is beautiful, but it can also be a frightening, crushing, exhausting thing. Questioning whether you are good enough or up to the task. Always blaming yourself when things go wrong. Always being blamed.

I wonder, did Ersilia ever forgive herself for giving Natalina away? So often the hardest person to forgive, when you don't measure up to who or how you want to be, is yourself.

There exists a photograph, taken in 1948 at Trieste's Victory Lighthouse. It shows Natalina surrounded by family: her husband and three daughters, her son-in-law (my nonno) and all his extended family, including my mother. The occasion was a cousin's First Holy Communion. There were twenty-one people.

This photograph tells a happier story, that although Natalina may have lacked affection in her childhood, this didn't define her life. There is my great-grandmother, swathed at the end of her days in the love of her own family.

It dawns on me that this is probably precisely the dream Ersilia had for her daughter, the reason she gave her away. It is unfortunate that Ersilia would never know any of this: how well Natalina's life worked out.

'Forgive, and you will be forgiven,' the Bible says. It's a reassuring thought, that if we dispense forgiveness, one day our children will forgive us our own shortcomings – and we might even be able to forgive ourselves.

I pick up that flipbook of Natalina's life again, and this time I play it forwards.

8
Enough

It was a simple document, pale blue with a white border and the city's crest. *'Certificato Di Morte'*. It was Ersilia's death certificate. I sat alone in a bar a short distance from Palazzo D'Accursio. The freshly printed page was set out on the table in front of me, beside a latte macchiato. I smoothed out where it had become wrinkled in my bag. The words had made me tear up when I'd read them in the municipal offices moments ago and I stared at them again now, half in disbelief. That I had obtained Ersilia's death certificate on this of all days, our last in Bologna, felt momentous.

She died on 1 April 1939, aged seventy-three. World War II had not yet reached Italy. Her older brother, Enrico, died in San Giovanni in Persiceto four weeks earlier. Mere coincidence? I pondered what that meant, whether it meant anything at all.

I had lodged the initial request for the certificate at the town hall at the start of the week, with the help of our Italian teacher. Obtaining a date of death would tell me for what period Ersilia's life intersected with Natalina's; I wanted to know how close her life had got to mine. Was Ersilia alive when my mother was born? Though too late for Natalina, it would still be closure for me to know when she died.

On that occasion I had approached D'Accursio not as a tourist but as a descendent of Bologna, carrying a stronger sense of attachment. Entering the building portal, I had glanced up at the imposing sixteenth-century bronze statue of Pope Gregory XIII (of Gregorian calendar fame). It was a symbolic moment, a reminder of the powers that shaped the destinies of so many single women and their babies, and of why I was there. Inside, a clerk told us that the information we sought, because it was historical, could take a long time to retrieve. We said I'd be leaving Bologna at the weekend, so she suggested I come back on Friday, just in case.

It would take a minor miracle, I had muttered to Valentina as we left, for the registry to locate the death certificate in such a short time – Italian bureaucracy being notoriously cumbersome. Now here I was, four days later, sitting with the document before me. Even the clerk was surprised when she handed it over. '*Impossibile*', she'd said. As though Ersilia herself wanted me to have it. Afterwards, I propelled my wheelchair across all those cobblestones to the bar on my own, Michael and L having absconded to Giardini Margherita for one last play.

I imagined Ersilia on her death bed, thinking of the daughter she gave up. Did Natalina sense her mother's passing? Perhaps she experienced an odd sensation that spring day in 1939 and didn't know what it meant. Maybe she noticed a small bird on her windowsill or felt a soft breeze come from nowhere to gently caress her face. Natalina was forty-one; my nonna Anna was fifteen. It seemed incredible, but I had the sum of Ersilia's life: her beginning, the tragedy that underpinned her decision to relinquish her daughter, her end. I had reassembled a life, however sketchily, that none of the women in our lineage who came after were supposed to know.

I sent a text message to Milena, telling her my news. She replied that it was 'fate and faith' that I had found Ersilia's date of death. But I felt it was more than that. I believed it was Ersilia, reaching out from wherever spirits dwell, giving this paper to me, so I could close off her life. All we mortals coexist, those living and those already passed, only we do not always realise it.

Rilke in 'The First Elegy' wrote that it is wrong to distinguish too sharply between the living and the dead, when 'Angels (they say)' don't know the difference. Sitting at the bar on Via D'Azeglio, the street's busy end, it was utterly conceivable that Ersilia was here, sharing this other-worldly moment with me, two blocks from the foundling home, in the city where she took her last breath.

Natalina never knew her mother, and I never knew either of them. And yet the work I had done in reconstructing their stories made me the link between the pair, the only member of my family over many generations to have 'known' them both.

'All moments, past, present, and future, always have existed, always will exist.' It was science fiction, Kurt Vonnegut's Tralfamadorian concept of time. But the truth, as acknowledged in many non-Western cultures, is the past is never done.

Time is slippery. It is there for our own need for order and organisation, relative to the observer who measures it. Hence a clock on the floor runs more slowly than one on the table; people living in the mountains age faster than those living by the sea; a watch marks fewer seconds on the hand of someone who is moving. What is *real* lies beyond time.

In 'The Second Elegy' Rilke posed the question:

> Does the infinite space
> we dissolve into, taste of us then?

That word, 'taste', was so visceral, it made me squirm. As though if I opened my mouth and stuck out my tongue, minuscule remnants of the dead – ashes, bone fragments and the like – would settle there. But it also made me think about the marks that Ersilia had left, that were already present inside us, Natalina's descendants, inside me.

Entropy, the gradual decline into disorder, explains time's traces. Heat, which produces entropy, only travels in one direction. 'Only where there is heat is there a distinction between past and future,' writes Italian physicist Carlo Rovelli, a graduate of the University of Bologna. Like the writing of a pen on a page, the processing of a thought or the laying down of a memory, each act produces heat and without heat there would be no trace. Without traces, there would be no us.

It follows that just as the priest at San Giovanni in Persiceto scribbled Ersilia's name in 'The Book of Secret Baptisms' for me to find 120 years later, so too Ersilia's decision to give up Natalina left its imprint on my life. Ersilia thought she could disappear, could trick time, but she could not. She unknowingly left tracks that if you were not looking for them, you would not have known were there. She could not picture our faces, but if Ersilia gave away Natalina to save her, as the anthropologist on the terrace and the women in San Giovanni said, then she also saved all of us who came after: Anna, my mother, me. The fact that Natalina survived the foundling home when the odds were so stacked against her, and went on to marry and have daughters, meant that I was the very trace of a family that might never have been.

Before finding Ersilia, I knew of only three women who came before: my mother, Anna, and Natalina. Now there were six of us – with Ersilia, her mother, Enrica, and her grandmother Cristina – and I could keep going. I have a new starting point in my family tree on my mother's maternal side. I feel a satisfaction reading these new names. It tells me something about who I am. A chain links all us mothers; Ersilia's act of abandonment never broke that.

I thought of Sharon Olds's metaphor of her maternal line as a bouquet made up of her and her mother and her mother's mother and so on, the stem going 'down into an underground river'. My matriline was a child's posy collected from a wild field: irises, violets, dandelions. Our stems once reached down into a river; it was called the Samoggia. Sitting in the bar I knew this, but I hadn't before because that posy was held by a child who, running home clutching it for her mother, had tripped and some of the flowers had fallen out.

And so here we were, two women, my great-great grandmother and I, sharing this final moment of discovery over coffee in Bologna. Communing outside time, as though past and present had merged, sharing a story of things about which there was no memory, but for the one I had created.

I picked at a soft and buttery croissant, and watched Italians drink their espresso at the inside bar. Winter had arrived in Bologna and that morning workers in face masks were sprinkling salt in Piazza del Nettuno, but I had chosen an outside table because it was easier with the wheelchair. I was warm enough, inside the prefabricated enclosure on the pavement. I admired the red walls, the stained-glass ceiling with orange sunflowers. Travellers pulled their overnight bags along Via D'Azeglio, and the noise of the wheels clip-clopping across the paving stones sounded like horses in another era. A young woman in a red beret passed by with a large shaggy dog on a lead; a pharmacy sign opposite flashed green.

Then a more familiar figure appeared, the old, stooped man with his walking stick and holy cards. His eyes, as always, were fixed on the ground, probably so he wouldn't trip over the raised edge of a cobblestone or the tattered hems of his trousers. I watched him shuffle past in the direction of Piazza Maggiore, a wooden cross dangling from his neck. A shop assistant had told me the man's name. He was from Eastern Europe and wouldn't divulge more about himself, possibly because like most of Bologna's beggars he was controlled by a ringleader and afraid of punishment.

Beggars were a constant presence in Bologna. It was as though each one held up a mirror to your soul. I recalled a recent scene we witnessed after a meal on Strada Maggiore, part of Via Emilia, the ancient Roman road.

We had just exited the bar when we saw an elderly woman emerge from a Coop supermarket with a trolley bag. I noticed her because the bag was just like the one my nonna, Anna, used to haul her shopping home, up her hilly street in Campsie in south-west Sydney. Suddenly the woman stopped and opened the bag's flap. She had come upon a beggar and now reached into the bag, pulling out a selection of grocery items, a packet of pasta and the like, and handed them to the man. Then she closed her trolley and resumed her journey along the street.

How often did the woman do this, I wondered: after every shop? Or was it a spontaneous display of compassion? Her action felt redemptive, a reminder of humankind's capacity to surprise in ways that are good. With all that I was discovering about Ersilia's life, it came as a salve.

When Ersilia was an elderly woman of seventy years, she moved to Bologna. She was following her son, Paolino, who had relocated there nine years prior. At the time of Ersilia's death, she was living with Paolino, his wife and their two sons on Vicolo Paglia Corta, 'Short Straw Lane'. The street name made me smile, as though it hid a secret joke (it was named for the straw warehouses that supplied Bologna's stables). I speculated about that long separation from her son, the years on her own in San Giovanni, when she missed watching her grandsons grow up. I could never know if hers and Paolino's remained a harmonious relationship; what, for example, she told him of his 'unknown' father or his missing sister. But I found fragments of Ersilia's and Paolino's shared life and pieced together the key events that preceded his permanent departure from San Giovanni.

The year 1915 was eventful. Ersilia's father, Teodoro, finally died the month Italy declared war on Austria-Hungary and, a few months later, her son was called to arms. Paolino's military record revealed he served three years with the *Automobilisti* company in the horse artillery regiment stationed in Mantua, Lombardy, on the front line. At twenty-four, he gave his profession as typographer. Like Natalina, he was short with straight black hair, black eyes and dark colouring.

I pictured him in his kepi-style military cap, the grey-green Italian uniform, the black stand collar with white stars, farewelling his mother at the train station. I imagined Ersilia's fear, thinking she was going to lose another child, the son she lived for. Her fears would only have intensified when the telegrams began arriving – hundreds of them, descending on the town like a plague of locusts. San Giovanni lost 334 men in World War I.

This time, God was merciful. Paolino survived, though Ersilia still lost him in a way, to the other woman who had been nervously awaiting his return: his San Giovanni–born fiancée. I worked this out from a note scrawled in the margins of his secret baptismal record. Paolino departed the territory of war one week before Armistice Day. Less than a fortnight after leaving the battlefield, the twenty-seven-year-old married his sweetheart, the young woman whose photograph he probably kept tucked in an inside pocket. He didn't waste a minute upon his return. The pair married on 17 November 1918 in the Santa Maria della Pietra church in Bologna. Little did Paolino know that his sister resided four streets from the church.

Ersilia's move to Bologna in 1935 was curious for another reason. It brought her permanently within a kilometre of the foundling home. She would have been unaware that, by then, her daughter had moved to Trieste, and I wondered if she ever tried to picture the girl as a grown woman, searched crowds for her face? Did she sometimes find herself on Via D'Azeglio struck by an urge to keep walking, as though her legs had a will of their own? I pictured her standing with her back to the San Procolo church, staring at the long portico across the road, wondering if it had all been worth it.

Natalina's foundling home file contained a puzzling entry. In 1912, when she was thirteen, someone opened a bank account for her, depositing five lire. The archivists could not explain who might have done this (it was not the millers). A redemptive act of love, perhaps? I could only think of one person.

I had been at the bar for two hours and decided to order a wine. A couple of English tourists arrived, took a nearby table and opened a guidebook. I saw the page they were reading from, about the terracotta sculptures at Santa Maria della Vita, with their frozen, anguished faces.

We had visited the baroque church. It was said the fifteenth-century artist Niccolò dell'Arca studied the faces of the bereaved and the dying for his work *Lamentation over the Dead Christ*. The women's grief, his mother's, was primeval: mouths open, teeth bared, fingers gripping thighs. It made you want to cry out with them. It made me think of my mother, keeping a vigil in the intensive care unit as doctors removed my legs.

I wished I could share with Ersilia what became of Natalina, how she shifted to Trieste in her early twenties, met her husband and made a family of her own. The resilience she showed, some of which has passed down to me. I imagined Ersilia sitting on the empty chair at my table, and me reassuring her that her daughter's life had turned out okay. 'You would have been so proud of her pluck, the way she fashioned a destiny out of so little,' I would say.

How Natalina came to meet Antonio was a source of curiosity to the Bologna archivists. It was uncommon, they said, for unmarried women still legally connected to the foundling home to leave Bologna to work in a distant part of Italy (Trieste being 300 kilometres away).

Being motherless – unencumbered by parents, family, village – meant Natalina was alone in the world, but she was also free. This must have felt terrifying yet liberating, not knowing how life would unfold in Trieste, with no real family to return to should things not work out.

When I returned home after working in London in my mid-twenties, encumbered by a hefty credit card debt, I lived for a few months in my parents' attic, in a room my father built especially for me so I could have a space of my own.

Trieste of the early interwar years was a restless, disoriented place. With the end of Austro-Hungarian rule, the city lost its purpose as one of the Empire's most significant ports. Authorities were grappling to control huge flows of people: returning soldiers, from both sides of the war, and Italians pouring in from the south. It was in such a time and place – 1922, the year fascists took control in Italy – that the union between Natalina and Antonio was forged.

Natalina met Antonio one day while out walking her boss's dog in a park. I tried to imagine the park, wished I could find it. I had Natalina's address from her correspondence with the foundling home regarding her engagement: Via SS Martiri, care of the Rizzo family, close to the port.

The proximity to the port rang true since her boss was a sea captain. The sea in Trieste is omnipresent. Its briny smell is blown into the streets by the frequent winds; its sound is carried by the squawking gulls that echo in the empty spaces between buildings.

From old index cards at Trieste's municipal offices, I discovered a little about the Rizzo sisters at number twenty-five. Giudita and Ermenegilda were 'housewives' in their mid-forties. Not originally from Trieste, they occupied a first-floor apartment where they housed several younger nieces and nephews and took in lodgers like Natalina for extra money. From census information at the Archivio Generale, I also found the sea captain boss. Francesco Scopinich was a forty-one-year-old bachelor, occupation *capitano mercante*, 'merchant captain', who lived with his sister and her family in the same building, the next floor up.

It turned out Antonio lived on Natalina's street, at number twenty-eight.

One cloudy afternoon in Trieste we went looking for Via SS Martiri: Michael, L, my mother and me. The street, whose name referenced an ancient cemetery for early Christian martyrs, was steep and winding and lined either side with modern apartment blocks. Neither of their house numbers existed any longer. However, at the bottom of the hill, I found what I was really looking for: a small park inhabited by tall trees, children chasing pigeons – and people walking dogs.

Giardino di Piazza Hortis was bordered by a low stone wall, where a busker sat playing the piano accordion. At the entrance stood a bronze statue of Triestine writer Italo Svevo, whose English teacher was famously James Joyce. While my son explored the children's playground, I followed the park's gravel paths and timber boardwalks. All the trees had labels: Mediterranean cypress, horse chestnut, Himalayan cedar, London plane, English yew, holly oak, empress tree, green olive, European nettle. Parks were a rarity in Trieste. Given this one's proximity to Natalina's house, it had to be where she walked the captain's dog, where she and Antonio met and fell in love.

Antonio was two years younger than Natalina, with light-brown hair that matched his eyes and a reddish complexion, according to his World War I records. Called up to the Italian Army when he turned eighteen, in the war's final year, it's unlikely he saw much action. Antonio's forebears were Austrian, and he spoke German. His maternal grandfather, Heinrich Barwig, was a tax collector from the district of Nový Jičín, Sigmund Freud's birthplace. Once ruled by the Habsburgs, today it sits in the Czech Republic, a three-hour drive from Vienna. Heinrich migrated to Trieste sometime around 1860, after the southern railway linking the city to Vienna was built.

I imagined Antonio's and Natalina's first meeting. It was a mild spring afternoon; Antonio may have bent down to pat the captain's dog as it sniffed at a gnarly tree. Natalina, wearing a simple, dark, loose-fitting dress and a religious pendant around her neck, would have seen a good-looking man with high cheekbones and a heart-shaped face (like his mother's). When he stood up again, she barely reached his shoulders. Perhaps the pair walked back up the hill together, the dog trotting along between them on its lead.

Antonio proposed in the hot summer of 1923. What a moment it would have been for Natalina, who had never experienced love before. In this man she saw her longed-for future unfurl like a flower that takes years to bloom: a name, a home, a family of her own. (Is it any wonder she worshipped him slavishly?)

The wedding took place in the late autumn at Beata Vergine del Soccorso, 'Blessed Virgin of Succour'. It is a simple church with a single nave, a stone floor and a yellow beeswax-colour exterior, whose history can be traced back to a legendary visit to Trieste by Saint Anthony of Padua in the 1200s. The church is separated from Giardino di Piazza Hortis by a narrow one-lane road. Was Antonio's disapproving family somewhere in the pews? Antonio had lost his father, a mechanic from Udine, by then. His mother, solemn-faced and wearing mourning dress in the only photograph that exists of her, and his older sister, who married into money, were alive but disapproved of his choice of bride. I applauded my great-grandfather, who married his foundling *amore* anyway.

Finding that park! My mother hadn't known it existed – and it was where her grandparents first met. I was overjoyed; she was underwhelmed. But it didn't matter, not really. Sharing that moment with her, I wrote in my journal, was 'heaven'. 'It makes it so much more meaningful.'

And that correspondence with the foundling home about her engagement? The letters were kept at Bologna's provincial archives in an old brown box tied with string. Their subject was the dowry to which Natalina was entitled, and they represented the foundling home's final act as her 'father' before it passed responsibility to Antonio (women always being owned by someone).

Holding the originals in my hand that day in Bologna was like holding star dust. I could hardly believe these precious artefacts – the letters of a foundling girl on the cusp of breaking free of the institution that had owned her since the day she was born – had been preserved all this time. I imagined describing them to Ersilia, as if they were her child's glowing school report.

'Ersilia, you would have been impressed by your daughter's letters to the foundling home director requesting her dowry,' I would say. 'The way she wrote *Bologna* on the envelopes – in curly cursive with exaggerated loops and thick black ink – seemed confident and dreamy. Like somebody in love.'

Then I would share one with her, pointing out Natalina's unmistakeable tone: respectful, assertive. I would explain the underlying sense of frustration, how Antonio had proposed months earlier; the foundling home was clearly dithering.

> Trieste, 17 August 1923
> Dear Mr Director
> Please be so kind as to give me an explanation as to how I should go about getting my dowry that I am entitled to. Since I want to get married and have all the necessary documents ready, but without your consent I cannot do anything . . .

'Like a father,' Ersilia would tell me. 'The foundling home needed as much information as possible about the prospective husband before granting its blessing.'

'Boxes had to be ticked,' I would agree. 'The body governing Bologna's hospitals had to be advised. The foundling home needed Antonio's police check.'

Pulling out another letter, I would say, 'See here. Natalina must have sent them what they needed, then wrote to them again.'

> Trieste, 29 September 1923
> Dear Mr Director
> I implore you to send me back the police check, as soon as it is verified, because my fiancé needs it. I hope now you have all the papers, which I sent to you, and I do not have to wait any longer for what is due to me . . .

'Reading Natalina's letters,' I would tell Ersilia, 'you may be struck, as I was, how Natalina did not think of herself as a victim of her birth circumstances, a passive actor waiting to be rescued. She was a confident and resourceful young woman with agency.'

I would tell her the director gave his consent to the marriage that October. That the final piece of internal correspondence was his handwritten letter two months later, confirming Natalina and Antonio were officially married, and requesting the dowry be paid through the Trieste municipal authority.

I would then place the letters on the table and look Ersilia in the eye.

'From these letters, you must see,' I would say, 'how abandoning your daughter gave her a dowry she never would have had otherwise. If this was your motivation all along, your plan came to fruition. By relinquishing Natalina, you gave her possibilities that were unrestrained by your own family's situation and trajectory. You could not have known at the time whether what you did would ultimately confer blessings or curses upon Natalina, but I believe it was the former.'

And then I would apologise.

Some weeks before that final day in Bologna, we had visited Biblioteca Salaborsa, the city's public library, a spacious and light-filled pavilion built on top of Roman ruins which could be viewed through transparent panels in the floor. While L played in the Salaborsa Ragazzi, the children's reading room, a librarian helped me locate the collection of books about the Bastardini hospital. One book was especially illuminating. Published on the 100th anniversary of papal rule ending, it charted the changes to regulations for unwed mothers over the centuries the Bastardini operated.

During the time of the Papal State, an unwed mother was forbidden to keep her child.

From 1862, following Italian Unification, if she wanted to keep the baby the midwife could not oppose it.

After World War I, staff had 'to make every effort, in the most loving manner, to persuade the mother to acknowledge her child'.

After World War II, officials confidently declared 'single mothers were no longer subject to all of the prejudices of the past'.

In 1960, it was recognised that denying illegitimate children their mothers' love was deeply damaging to their development.

I was struck by the vulnerability of these women, who were at the mercy of shifting religious, social and political sensibilities regarding their suitability for motherhood.

I saw hints of Ersilia in Toni Morrison's *Beloved*, a novel I first read in my late teens, about an escaped slave in mid-nineteenth-century America who murdered her baby daughter to prevent her being returned to slavery. She was later haunted by the child's angry ghost. The mother was accused of having love that was 'too thick' – that is, of loving too much.

How else can a mother love, I wondered, other than thickly?

Ersilia was faced with an agonising choice. I have no doubt now that she did what she thought was best for her daughter. At the beginning of my investigations into Natalina's abandonment, I asked what kind of mother would forsake her child. Now I believed I knew: a total mother who loved thickly, as fiercely as a lioness with her cubs.

The waiter brought me my glass of red wine, some olives and potato crisps. I explained that I was waiting for my husband and son. As he poured the wine, two drops fell onto the death certificate, staining it red.

'Try,' the waiter told me, and obediently I sipped the wine.

Earlier in the week we visited the hairdressing studio that had just opened next door to our apartment on Via Parigi. The salon was furnished with a red sofa and white laminate floorboards. I had taken a seat in a brand-new salon chair in front of a gilded wall mirror, and told the owner, Martina, in my best Italian that I wanted to go red – really red.

Martina was young, with long dark hair and red lipstick. While she smothered my hair in a thick paste, she told me she was from a small island off Sicily and moved to Bologna to learn a different mentality of working. It was difficult setting up her own shop, but in general the Bolognese were friendlier than Italians further north. In Milan, for instance, if you fell over in the street the Milanese would check out your outfit and leave you there. Whereas in Bologna, people didn't care how you dressed and would help you up off the ground.

Several hours later my short locks were shockingly red, as red as the Ferraris we took our car-mad son to see at Maranello.

Now sipping my wine as I waited for my husband and son to join me from the park, I recalled that first meal in Bologna, how alien I had felt in the city. It struck me how – with my new hair, extra kilos, and deeper knowledge of Bologna's foundling history – I had become Natalina's city embodied: red, fat and learned.

Are our expectations of maternal love unrealistic? Are mine? I could yearn all I like for a 'deeper' relationship with my mother, or I could accept that she loves me the only way she is capable of, because that's all we mothers can do.

My mother shows me her love whenever she takes a new pair of trousers for me to the tailor to get them taken up, so they fit the prosthetics. Or deposits my unwanted books in the street library across our busy road. Or returns an online shopping parcel to the post office for me. Or buys my son the mortadella he loves from her local Italian delicatessen. Or finds me a cleaner for my house and a nurse because my scars have opened again. Or makes me chicken soup when I'm sick. Or cuts back the neighbour's wisteria so it doesn't engulf our roof. She showed me her love when I said I wished I could try *presnitz*, the Triestine nut-and-raisin-filled strudel Natalina used to make (which Joyce himself was known to like), and she immediately baked me one. My mother finds it difficult to articulate her love for me in words; the expressions 'how are you, really?' or 'I love you' do not come easily. She is a fixer, a doer, a woman of boundless energy, a woman of action. She sees me encounter a problem and tries to solve it.

Arriving in Bologna, I was riven by maternal doubt about Ersilia's mothering because of her abandonment of Natalina, and about mine because of my disability. But doubt hollows out and weakens, like a fruit tree punctured by boring insects. It is wearying, to run yourself down all the time, to feel that you are never enough. In trying to understand Ersilia, I realised something about myself: how urgent my own need for self-forgiveness is. Uncovering her shame, I found my own.

Having once asked what kind of mother Ersilia was, I tried to answer it about myself.

I am an older mother of one son. A mother who writes, gardens, swims, and cries at the football.

A mother who has never driven her son to school but has read with him almost every night of his life. A mother whose left leg plugs into an electric socket to recharge overnight; a mother who loves to walk beside her son, but doesn't very often. A mother whose wheelchair squeaks and clunks, most annoyingly when she's trying to exit her son's room quietly after he has finally fallen asleep (this doesn't annoy the son, however, who tells her that, to his ears, the sound is 'musical').

A mother who misses her old body and often feels alienated from the world because of what happened to her. Who tries not to take this out on the people she loves most, but does not always succeed. A mother who worries, is too hard on herself and others, but never stops trying to be otherwise, who admits when she has made a mistake.

I have a creed, four words, for when motherhood is overwhelming me, and I need to remind myself what matters: 'You are my heart.'

It happened once these past weeks during homeschooling. One morning, L refused to write in the journal his teacher back at home had suggested – I had envisaged it being a keepsake of his time in Italy, but it was mostly about Minecraft – and started to cry. I was exhausted.

'You are my heart,' I said, ripping off a huge chunk of panettone, the only thing I believed in that moment could make me feel better.

'You are ten times my heart,' L replied.

'You are one hundred times my heart,' I said, now smiling.

'You are one hundred times my life,' said my son.

Re-reading aloud 'The First Elegy' one day, I experienced an exhilarating moment of insight. It was as fleeting as a birthday candle being lit in a draught. I madly scribbled down notes, trying to capture what I had just grasped. The elegy touches on the strangeness of death.

I saw the dead Ersilia, the woman who wouldn't be named, in the words:

> to leave
> even one's own first name behind, forgetting it
> as easily as a child abandons a broken toy.

I saw my insecure self, always doubting my mothering, my worth, in the line:

> to be
> what one was in infinitely anxious hands …

And I saw, most startlingly, what connected us. That, in the end, the dead 'no longer need us'. The more apposite question I should have been asking was whether:

> we for whom grief is so often
> the source of our spirit's growth –: could we exist without
> *them*?

These last words caught in my throat as I pronounced them to the empty room. I marvelled at how Rilke could have captured so perfectly the nexus between Ersilia and me. And yet, writing in 1912 at the old Duino Castle, which sits on a rocky outcrop overlooking the Gulf of Trieste, he did. It is the living who need the dead to make sense of their difficult, chaotic, fearful lives. The passive, timeless dead. I had to piece together the shards of Ersilia's broken, troubling story because I needed to learn what it means to be a mother, so that I might forgive my own maternal failings – and understand that sometimes the failings aren't necessarily my own, but society's.

I think of how I feel when a mum sees me sitting alone at a mothers' lunch for my son's year, while the other mums interact on their feet, and asks to join me. How I feel when a mother I befriended at that lunch asks, six months later, if I'd like to go to an art gallery event with parents from our son's year, then calls ahead to arrange a disabled parking spot for us.

I feel surprised, grateful, reassured when I am given opportunities to make social connections that will enrich our son's life. I feel like any other mother.

What a difference it would make if school leaders – leaders of any organisations with parental involvement in children's experiences – decreed it a core value to consider those with disability in their communities. It would mean such parents don't have to decide every time: should I ask about accessibility, potentially causing the organisers to have to alter their plans for me, drawing attention to myself? Or should I just not go at all?

I was the one who needed Ersilia, not she who needed me. Such a complicated thing it is to love your child.

My son does not ask me about my injuries very often. There are times I wish I could read what passes through his mind, to know whether it troubles him when his life is curtailed by, and has to be arranged around, my needs as a disabled mum. So I was surprised when one night back in Sydney, as I was tucking him into bed, he asked me what I liked about being in a wheelchair.

'Nothing,' I replied instantly. 'There is nothing I like about being in a wheelchair.'

Then I stopped and thought about it.

'Nothing except for this,' I added. 'That when you were little, we got to ride together. First when you were with me, sitting on my lap. And later when you were beside me, riding your scooter, like we did along the porticoes in Bologna.'

It was now lunchtime and I checked my iPhone for messages. There was one from Michael; he and L were on their way. I pulled out the menu to order them sandwiches; the local *piadine*, flat bread, looked good.

It occurred to me that maybe Ersilia already knew everything I had told her about her daughter. That Natalina may have found her in the afterlife, that they might be together now, with Paolino and his family, with my nonna and her sisters.

Silently, I thanked Ersilia for her story. Unexceptional, unromantic. At times so ugly I wanted to turn away. Yet defiant, hopeful. Through it, I understood more about my female lineage, about how we mothered. I learnt that at its core was how we survived as women, and how – despite the cards dealt to us – we loved as women, and as mothers.

My husband and son arrived at the bar. I pulled out the death certificate and recounted my findings to them. They ate their sandwiches and then we returned to the apartment for our final night in Bologna, me in my wheelchair, L beside me on his scooter, Michael walking behind us.

And I knew that I loved my boy as completely as I could, constrained in my actions but never my words, and that was enough.

Acknowledgements

I would like to thank the people who helped with the research of this book. To Milena Selivanov, for accepting the assignment all those years ago: for your enthusiasm, time, skill and dedication. Spending that week in Bologna with you will always be a treasured memory. To Valentina Ferrari and your boys, for taking my family under your wing and teaching us about your beloved city. To all the archivists, especially Dr Letizia Bongiovanni and Dr Francesco Rosa at the Archivio Storico Provinciale, who helped me make sense of Natalina's life. To the generous women in San Giovanni in Persiceto who helped locate Natalina's mother and shared their knowledge of secret baptisms with me. Thank you Dr Chiara Reatti, Milena Turchi, Giuseppina Bosi, Patrizia Fiorini, Maria Pia Montori. To the wonderful people I met in Gaggio Montano: Margarete Bunje, Adelfo Cecchelli, Mauro Brunetti. I would especially like to thank Giuseppe Mingarelli for sharing your story with me. To the Bolognese anthropologists and historians who spoke to me about foundlings, who wish to remain nameless. To the librarians at Biblioteca Salaborsa in Bologna, Biblioteca Comunale E. De Amicis in Anzola Dell'Emilia, Biblioteca Comunale 'Giulio Cesare Croce' in San Giovanni in Persiceto, and Biblioteca Civica Attilio Hortis in Trieste for answering all my questions. To Facts & Files, especially Sabine Altmann, for helping track down family records. To Sandra Paulovic, and the hospitable owners of La Porta Rossa. To Italian Connections, for translating Italian texts, including interviews, academic works and archival documents. And to David Kertzer, whose work on Bologna's foundlings gave me invaluable context to Natalina's story.

I would like to thank the people who believed in, supported and provided feedback on this work. To Nadine Davidoff, for your perceptive suggestions and for encouraging me not to give up. To Mary-Jane Holmes, your mentoring was indispensable. To Dasom Yang for nurturing my writing. I would also like to thank Varuna, the National Writer's House, for letting me use part of my Writer's Space Fellowship to write an early chapter in the wonderful, accessible Jerra Studio. Also to the teachers I met through Varuna and Writing NSW who offered me guidance and feedback: Lee Kofman, Carol Major, Sisonke Msimang. To my supportive online writing group: Belinda Pratten, Kathy Prokhovnik, Anna Fursland, Maggie Walters, Rachel Eldred. To Marion Frith, Michele Smart, Paul Daley, Emily Tannock for your friendship and writing advice. And to Terri-ann White, heartfelt thanks for taking on my manuscript.

Finally, this book involves the stories of living people. Writing about them was not easy. It raised tricky questions of privacy, ownership. Who owns stories about family, including ones told to us, that we didn't personally experience? When those stories help us to understand what made us, do they become ours? What right do we have to tell stories about our children? As writers we make these decisions governed by our own moral compasses. Writing this book, the sense of moral duty weighed heavily – towards family members, my readers, and myself – to tell the most truthful story I could without causing unnecessary hurt. It was a difficult balancing act. I would like to thank the people whose love sustained me during the research and writing of this work. To my parents. Especially my mother, because you are my mother, and because without you, I will always feel less.

And to Michael and L: you are my world.

Some Sources

1: Judgement

(Slaughterhouses) – Kertzer, D.I. and M.J. White, 'Cheating the angel-makers: surviving infant abandonment in nineteenth-century Italy', *Continuity and Change*, vol. 9, 1994, pp. 451–80.

Olds, S., 'Grey Girl', *The Unswept Room*, New York: Alfred A. Knopf, 2012, pp. 19–20.

(Napoleon, Madonna's protection, midwives' homes) – Kertzer, D.I., *Sacrificed for Honor: Italian Infant Abandonment and the Politics of Reproductive Control*, Boston: Beacon Press, 1993.

Wright, C.D., 'Our Dust', *Steal Away: Selected and New Poems*, Port Townsend: Copper Canyon Press, 2003, pp. 73–74.

(Wheels by 1875) – Viazzo, P.P., M. Bortolotto and A. Zanotto, 'Five centuries of foundling history in Florence: changing patterns of abandonment, care and mortality' in C. Panter-Brick and M.T. Smith, *Abandoned Children*, New York: Cambridge University Press, 2000, pp. 70–91.

(Wheel in 1873) – Rubbi, U. and C. Zucchini, 'L'Ospizio Esposti e L'Asilo di Maternità', in Dell'Amministrazione degli Ospedali di Bologna (ed.), *Sette Secoli di Vita Ospitaliera in Bologna*, Bologna: Cappelli Editore, 1960, pp. 401–17.

Hartman, S., *Lose Your Mother: A Journey Along the Atlantic Slave Route*, London: Serpent's Tail, 2021.

2: Margins

Boulton, S., *Bologna Pocket Guide*, London: APA Publications, 2016.

(*Gettatelli*) – Lenci, M., 'Rinominarsi nell'Ottocento e nel Novecento', in A. Addobbati, R. Bizzocchi and G. Salinaro, *L'Italia dei Cognomi. L'antroponimia Italiana nel Quadro Mediterraneo*, Pisa: Pisa University Press, 2012, pp. 567–83.

(Most common surnames) – Kertzer, D.I., H. Koball and M.J. White, 'Growing up as an abandoned child in nineteenth-century Italy', *The History of the Family*, 1997, vol. 2, pp. 211–28.

(*Pio luogo*) – Fanti, M., 'L'Ospedale di San Procolo o dei Bastardini tra Medioevo e Rinascimento', in Amministrazione Provinciale di Bologna Assessorato alla Cultura, *I Bastardini: Patrimonio e Memoria di un Ospedale Bolognese*, Bologna: Edizioni Age, 1990, pp. 7–38.

(Protestantism, sanctioned anonymous abandonment, River Tiber, third of all babies) – Kertzer, *Sacrificed for Honor.*

(Six per cent, economic crisis) – Kertzer, D.I. and D.P. Hogan, *Family, Political Economy, and Demographic Change: The Transformation of Life in Casalecchio, Italy, 1861–1921*, Madison: The University of Wisconsin Press, 1989.

(Pellagra) – Ginnaio, M., 'Pellagra in late nineteenth-century Italy: effects of a deficiency disease', *Population*, 2011, vol. 66, pp. 583–610.

Hartman, S., 'Venus in two acts', *Small Axe*, vol. 26, 2008, pp. 1–14.

3: Instincts

(not an offensive term, *Stelline*) – Sirgi, G., *I Bastardini: Figli di Donne che non Vollero essere Nominate*, Porretta Terme: Gruppo di Studi Alta Valle Del Reno, 1994.

(Angels' wings) – Terpstra, N., *Abandoned Children of the Italian Renaissance: Orphan Care in Florence and Bologna*, Baltimore: John Hopkins University Press, 2005.

Ford, R., *Between Them: Remembering My Parents*, London: Bloomsbury Publishing, 2017.

Enright, A., *The Wren, The Wren*, London: Jonathan Cape, 2023.

(Emergency baptism powers, nursed multiple) – Kertzer, *Sacrificed for Honor.*

(House of Correction) – Fronzoni, S., 'Lontano dalla madre. Forme e istituti della esposizione a Bologna nella prima metà dell'ottocento', *Sanità Scienza e Storia*, no. 2, 1989, pp. 55–76.

(Conditions inside, killing children) – Kertzer, D.I. and M.J. White, 'Cheating the angel-makers: surviving infant abandonment in nineteenth-century Italy'.

Plath, S., 'Tulips', *Ariel*, London: Faber & Faber, 1965, pp. 20–22.

(Invisible thread) – Rich, A., *Of Woman Born: Motherhood as Experience and Institution*, New York: W.W. Norton & Company, 1986, 2021.

(Preferred sharecroppers) – Kertzer, D.I., W. Sigle and M.J. White, 'Childhood mortality and quality of care among abandoned children in nineteenth-century Italy', *Population Studies*, vol. 53, 1999 pp. 303–15.

(One-in-four, three months to place, 474 babies) – Kertzer, D.I., 'Syphilis, foundlings, and wetnurses in nineteenth-century Italy', *Journal of Social History*, vol. 32, 1999, pp. 589–602.

(Sued the Bastardini) Kertzer, D.I., *Amalia's Tale: A Poor Peasant, An Ambitious Attorney, and a Fight for Justice*, New York: Houghton Mifflin, 2008.

(*Stanza della ruota*, Bentivoglio) – Fanti, M., 'L'Ospedale di San Procolo o dei Bastardini tra Medioevo e Rinascimento'.

Hunt, E., 'Lily Grace inquest: coroner recommends use of "baby boxes" at hospitals', *The Guardian*, 10 February 2016.

4: Inheritance

Jodorowsky A. and M. Costa, *Metagenealogy: Self-Discovery through Psychomagic and the Family Tree*, translated by R. LeValley, Rochester: Park Street Press, 2011, 2014.

Tamaro, S., *Listen to My Voice*, translated by J. Cullen, London: Harvill Secker, 2008.

(Turned fifteen) – Stefanizzi, D., 'L'Ospedale di San Procolo o dei Bastardini di Bologna', in G. Greco, *Criminalità e Controllo Sociale a Bologna nell-Ottocento*, Bologna: Pàtron Editore, 1998, pp. 161–70.

(Responsible for their honour) – Kertzer, D.I. and W. Sigle, 'The marriage of female foundlings in nineteenth-century Italy', *Continuity and Change*, vol. 13, 1998, pp. 201–20.

(Making textiles) – Kertzer, *Sacrificed for Honor.*

Pagels, E., *Why Religion? A Personal Story*, New York: Ecco, 2018, 2020.

5: Perspectives

Messbarger, R., 'Re-membering a body of work: Anatomist and anatomical designer Anna Morandi Manzolini', *Studies in Eighteenth-Century Culture*, vol. 32, 2003, pp. 123–54.

Andersen, H.C., *The Little Mermaid*, translated by M.R. James, London: Faber & Faber, 1953.

Alighieri, D., *Inferno: The Divine Comedy I*, translated by R. Kirkpatrick, London: Penguin Books, 2006.

6: Rupture

(*Braccianti*) – Sigle, W., D.I. Kertzer, M.J. White, 'Abandoned children and their transitions to adulthood in nineteenth-century Italy', *Journal of Family History*, vol. 25. 2000, pp. 326–40.

(Unhygienic lodgings) – Kertzer, D.I. and D.P. Hogan, *Family, Political Economy, and Demographic Change: The Transformation of Life in Casalecchio*.

(Hemp work) Burani, M. and F. Fabbri (eds), *C'era Una Volta La Canapa … Immagini e Testimonianze*, Anzola Dell'Emilia: Comune di Anzola Dell'Emilia, 1997.

(Gethsemane) – Malaguti, D.A., *Il Bifolco: La Massaia e la Famiglia Contadina*, Bologna: Tamari Editori in Bologna, 1981.

(Female teacher) Biblioteca Edmondo de Amicis, 'Cronache Anzolesi 1860–1890', 2011, https://www.bibliotecanzola.it/cronache-anzolesi-1860-1890.

Ovid, *Metamorphoses*, translated by M.M. Innes, London: Penguin Books, 1955.

(Scraping away) Garuti, M., *La Memoria Dell'Acqua Nella Pianura Bolognese*, Bologna: Pendragon, 2008.

(Tiny grey flowers, watchman) Consulta di frazione Budrie–Castagnolo–Tivoli, *Il Samoggia e la Memoria: Testimonianze di Vita Dalle Borgate Fluviali sul Samoggia*, San Giovanni in Persiceto: Comune di San Giovanni in Persiceto, 1999.

(Child mortality, becoming widowed) – Kertzer, D.I. and D.P. Hogan, *Family, Political Economy, and Demographic Change: The Transformation of Life in Casalecchio*.

(Pointed shape) – Finelli, L., *Album d'Ifanzia da Fine Ottocento Agli Anno '50*, Anzola Dell'Emilia: Assessorato alla Cultura del Comune di Anzola Dell'Emilia, 1993.

(All domestic duties) Segalen, M., 'Material conditions of family life', in D.I. Kertzer and M. Barbagli (eds), *Family Life: In the Long Nineteenth Century 1789–1913*, New Haven: Yale University Press, 2002, pp. 3–39.

(Squalid accommodation) – Kertzer, D.I., 'Living with kin', in D.I. Kertzer and M. Barbagli (eds), *Family Life: In the Long Nineteenth Century 1789–1913*, pp. 40–72.

(Uncommonly late, pregnant brides) – Kertzer, D.I. and D.P. Hogan, *Family, Political Economy, and Demographic Change: The Transformation of Life in Casalecchio.*

Rilke, R.M., 'The Second Elegy', in *Duino Elegies and The Sonnets to Orpheus*, translated by S. Mitchell, New York: Vintage International, 1982, 2009, pp. 11–15.

7: Forgiveness

(Miller) Manicardi, N., *Il Grande Libro Dei Mestieri di una Volta: Artigianali, Ambulanti e Agricoli*, Finale Emilia: CDL, 2014.

(Cheap labour) – Dos Guimarães, I., 'Circulation of children in eighteenth-century Portugal', in C. Panter-Brick and M.T. Smith, *Abandoned Children*, pp. 27–40.

Sirgi, G., *I Bastardini: Figli di Donne che non Vollero essere Nominate.*

(Geographic mobility) – Kertzer, D.I. and D.P. Hogan, *Family, Political Economy, and Demographic Change: The Transformation of Life in Casalecchio.*

(Stability for children) – Kertzer, D.I., H. Koball and M.J. White, 'Growing up as an abandoned child in nineteenth-century Italy'.

8: Enough

Rilke, R.M., 'The First Elegy', in *Duino Elegies and The Sonnets to Orpheus*, translated by S. Mitchell, pp. 3–9.

Vonnegut, K., *Slaughterhouse-Five*, New York: Dell Publishing, 1969.

Rilke, R.M., 'The Second Elegy', in *Duino Elegies and The Sonnets to Orpheus*, translated by S. Mitchell.

Rovelli, C., *The Order of Time*, translated by E. Segre and S. Carnell, London: Penguin Books, 2018, 2019.

Olds, S., 'Pansy Glossary', *The Unswept Room*, p. 87.

(334 men) Storia e Memoria di Bologna, 'San Giovanni in Persiceto (BO) 1860–1918, Insediamento', 2000–2024, https://www.storiaememoriadibologna.it/archivio/luoghi/san-giovanni-persiceto-bo-2.

(Returning soldiers) – Amodeo, F., *Trieste: Una Storia per Immagini Volume 2: 1919–1932*, Trieste: La Biblioteca del Piccolo, 2004.

(Pouring in) – Apih, E., *Storia Delle Città Italiane: Trieste*, Bari: Editori Laterza, 1988.

(Vienna) – Apollonio, A., *La Ripresa Economica di Trieste Dopo il Ritorno Degli Asburgo e I Suoi Protagonisti (1814–1840)*, Trieste: Deputazione di Storia Patria per la Venezia Giulia, 2011.

(Southern Railway) – Botteri, G., *Una Storia Europea di Liberi Commerci e Traffici*, Trieste: Società Editoriale, 1988.

(Changes of regulations) – Rubbi, U. and C. Zucchini, 'L'Ospizio Esposti e L'Asilo di Maternità'.

Morrison, T., *Beloved*, London: Picador, 1987.

(*Presnitz*) – Crivelli, R.S., *Itinerari Triestini: James Joyce: Triestine Itineraries*, Trieste: MGS Press, 1996.

About Upswell

Upswell Publishing was established in 2021 by Terri-ann White as a not-for-profit press. A perceived gap in the market for distinctive literary works in fiction, poetry and narrative non-fiction was the motivation. In her years as a bookseller, writer and then publisher, Terri-ann has maintained a watch on literary books and the way they insinuate themselves into a cultural space and are then located within our literary and cultural inheritance. She is interested in making books to last: books with the potential to still be noticed, and noted, after decades and thus be ripe to influence new literary histories.

About this typeface

Book designer Becky Chilcott chose Foundry Origin not only as a strong, carefully considered, and dependable typeface, but also to honour her late friend and mentor, type designer Freda Sack, who oversaw the project. Designed by Freda's long-standing colleague, Stuart de Rozario, much like Upswell Publishing, Foundry Origin was created out of the desire to say something new.